Trouble In Paradise

A Humorous Story

HOW TO DEAL WITH PEOPLE
WHO PUSH YOUR BUTTONS

Using
TOTAL BRAIN COACHING

Robert Keith Wallace, PhD, Samantha Wallace, Ted Wallace, MS

© Copyright 2020 by Robert Keith Wallace, Samantha Wallace, Ted Wallace
All rights reserved.
Printed in the United States of America
No part of this publication may be reproduced, stored in a retrieval system, or transmitted in any form or by any means, electronic, mechanical, photocopying, recording, or otherwise, without prior written permission of the publisher.
Transcendental Meditation®, TM®, Maharishi®, Maharishi International University®, MIU®, and Maharishi AyurVeda® are protected trademarks and are used in the U.S. under license or with permission.
The advice and information in this book relates to health care and should be used to supplement rather than to replace the advice of your doctor or trained health professional. If you have any serious, acute, or chronic health concern, please consult a trained health professional who can fully assess your needs and address them effectively.
The publisher and authors disclaim liability for any medical outcomes as a result of applying any of the methods discussed in this book.

ISBN 978-0-9990558-9-2

Library of Congress Control Number: 2020917685

DharmaPublications.com

Dharma Publications, Fairfield, IA

To Our Very Dear Children and Grandchildren

OTHER BOOKS BY

Robert Keith Wallace, Samantha Wallace, and Ted Wallace

The Coherence Code
*How to Maximize Your Performance and Success in Business
For Individuals, Teams, and Organizations*
Robert Keith Wallace, PhD, Ted Wallace, MS,
Samantha Wallace

Total Brain Coaching
*A Holistic System of Effective Habit Change
For the Individual, Team, and Organization*
Ted Wallace, MS, Robert Keith Wallace, PhD,
Samantha Wallace

The Rest and Repair Diet
Heal Your Gut, Improve Your Physical and Mental Health, and Lose Weight
Robert Keith Wallace, PhD, Samantha Wallace,
Andrew Stenberg, MA, Jim Davis, DO, with Alexis Farley

Gut Crisis
*How Diet, Probiotics, and Friendly Bacteria
Help You Lose Weight and Heal Your Body and Mind*
Robert Keith Wallace, PhD, Samantha Wallace

Dharma Parenting
*Understand Your Child's Brilliant Brain for Greater
Happiness, Health, Success, and Fulfillment*
Robert Keith Wallace, PhD, Frederick Travis, PhD

Quantum Golf
The Path to Golf Mastery
NEW AND REVISED
Kjell Enhager, Robert Keith Wallace, PhD, Samantha Wallace

Beauty, Ayurveda, and Essential Oil Skincare
—A Friendly Introduction
Samantha Wallace, Robert Keith Wallace, PhD,
Veronica Wells Butler, MD

An Introduction to Transcendental Meditation
*Improve Your Brain Functioning, Create Ideal Health,
and Gain Enlightenment Naturally, Easily, Effortlessly*
Robert Keith Wallace, PhD, Lincoln Akin Norton

Transcendental Meditation
A Scientist's Journey to Happiness, Health, and Peace
Robert Keith Wallace, PhD

The Neurophysiology of Enlightenment
*How the Transcendental Meditation and TM-Sidhi Program
Transform the Functioning of the Human Body*
Robert Keith Wallace, PhD

Maharishi Ayurveda and Vedic Technology
Creating Ideal Health for the Individual and World
Robert Keith Wallace, PhD

The Coherence Effect
*Tapping into the Laws of Nature that Govern Health,
Happiness, and Higher Brain Functioning*
Robert Keith Wallace, PhD, Jay B. Marcus,
Christopher S. Clark, MD

CONTENTS

Cast of Characters..1

Prologue Paradise Lake..5

Prologue Commentary: Energy States.....................13

Chapter 1 Tippy Canoe...19

Chapter 1 Commentary: TBC Life Coaching............35

Chapter 2 The Black Hole of Calcutta.....................39

Chapter 2 Commentary: Karma...............................43

Chapter 3 Fatigue is the Enemy..............................45

Chapter 3 Commentary: DHARMIC..........................53

Chapter 4 The Hornets' Nest...................................57

Chapter 4 Commentary: Which Wolf Wins...............69

Chapter 5 The Bath From Hell.................................81

Chapter 5 Commentary: Maintaining Balance..........91

Chapter 6 The Honey Trap.....................................101

Chapter 6 Commentary: Fight or Flight..................111

Chapter 7 Damage Control....................................113

Chapter 7 Commentary: Types of Meditation..............................125

Epilogue The Peace Offering..129

Epilogue Commentary: Creating Coherence..................................135

Self Coaching 137

About the Authors..139

Acknowledgments...141

Resource Materials..143

Section 1 Energy State Characteristics.....................................145

Section 2 Meditation..157

Section 3 Gut-Brain Axis..169

Section 4 Self Pulse..171

Section 5 Habit Change..175

Section 6 Lifestyle Guidelines..179

Section 7 Health Coaching...187

Section 8 Beauty and Essential Oil Skincare................................191

Section 9 Relationship Coaching...193

Section 10 Parental Coaching..199

Section 11 Group Dynamics of Consciousness.................................205

Section 12. David Lynch Foundation..211

General References..213

Index..218

A SMITH FAMILY SAGA Book #3

CAST OF CHARACTERS

MR. SMITH

Our main character, J.P. Smith, first appeared in *Quantum Golf*. (Originally published in 1991, a revised edition will be available in 2021.) Smith is also the main character in *The Coherence Code*. And along with his wife, niece, and two sisters-in-law, he is featured in our latest book, *Beauty, Ayurveda, and Essential Oil Skincare—A Friendly Introduction*.

Mr. Smith is a typical busy businessman, whose enduring ambition is to improve his golf game.

[Note to Reader: Mr. Smith's frequent use of the words "Frakk" and "Frakking" has nothing to do with the process of hydraulic fracturing to obtain oil and gas, commonly known as fracking. It is merely the result of his viewing all 76 episodes of the television show *Battlestar Galactica* 7 times and counting.]

MARGARET

Margaret has been the love of Mr. Smith's life since they met in college and it is generally agreed that Smith hit the jackpot in his choice of wife. Margaret's deeply grounded nature, characteristic refinement, and strong intellect, along with her deep contentment with life, has a harmonizing influence on the entire family. People (and animals) tend to gravitate naturally towards Margaret and feel safe around her.

SERAPHIM

Seraphim is Margaret's older sister and the archenemy of J.P. Smith. She is a wealthy widow whose husband Freddie died several years ago. Seraphim dominates and misunderstands both of her younger siblings, Rose and Margaret, as well as her only child, Chloe.

[Note to Reader: The word "seraphim" is plural and means more than one seraph or angel. It may, therefore, seem odd to use "seraphim" to refer to a single person, but it is odder still that of the three sisters, she is one who bears the name of angels.]

CHLOE

Thirteen-year-old Chloe is as different in nature from Seraphim as any mother and daughter have ever been. Bright, creative, and refined, Chloe is Margaret and J.P.'s adored niece.

CHRIS TREVELYAN

Chris, or Uncle Chris as he is generally referred to, is a retired officer of the Royal Canadian Mounted Police. It is this wise and somewhat eccentric character who assumes the role of Smith's life coach.

LINC ST. CLAIRE

Linc St. Claire is a mystical golf teacher featured in both editions of *Quantum Golf*.

DAME GEORGINA ST. GEORGE

Georgina is Linc St. Claire's cousin. An extraordinary business consultant, who is much sought after by the rich and powerful, Dame Georgina appears in *The Coherence Code*.

TROUBLE IN PARADISE

PROLOGUE

Paradise Lake

"Why do we have to go all the way to Quebec to be with your infernal sister?" J.P. Smith grumbles, not for the first time, as their late model Lexus SUV moves with almost embarrassing smoothness over the lumpy, bumpy gravel road.

"Dar-ling," she says, "I told you, it's Seraphim's seventieth birthday."

Seraphim—the name makes him shudder. *Why,* he asks himself, *did I ever agree to visit this northern wilderness to celebrate the birth of my own nemesis? Just because she is Margaret's big sister doesn't change the fact that the woman chews glass and breathes fire!*

"It's in the middle of nowhere, Margaret. What will I do?" He knows that he sounds like a whiny kid, but he continues, "I bet there isn't a golf course within 100 miles."

"You can go rowing and canoeing!" Margaret says. "My sisters and I spent the happiest part of our childhood here. I always loved being out on the lake."

They have been driving for hours...*I must have been out of my mind to agree to this,* he thinks, but says nothing.

Here and there small towns emerge from the forest and a few blocks later, disappear into the mostly pine and maple woods, until at last they arrive at Paradise Lake. For years Smith has heard about it from Margaret and her sisters, and now he catches blue glimpses through the trees as the GPS announces that they have reached their final destination.

Smith stares at a cluster of vintage cottages on both sides of the road.

"It hasn't changed in forty years," Margaret announces happily as they get out of the car.

I can well believe it, he says to himself, unloading their bags. But the cottages are nicely painted and the roofs look sound. *Still, they could be a hundred years old. And nothing like the places I usually stay in on my golf outings.*

A thought claws his brain: *What if there's no indoor plumbing?*

As they enter the front door of the main cabin, they can see all the way into the living room and through a glassed-in porch to the lake beyond.

Margaret cries, "Look at that view!" and squeezes his arm, but he isn't ready to commit himself. He walks behind her as she explores large and small changes in the house and is greatly relieved to pass a door which clearly leads to a bathroom. *At this point in my life, an outhouse would be too much.*

When they go into the sunroom, he has to admit that yes, it's a beautiful lake—surrounded by trees and with relatively few houses along its shore. But he's not sold. *In my book, the primary purpose of a body of water is to serve as a golf hazard!*

The couple decide to unpack but before they finish, their 13-year-old niece Chloe appears at the door. "Welcome to Shangri-La," she says cheerfully, holding her slender arms out to hug them.

"Or in your case, Uncle John," she says to Smith, "welcome to the home of your prime adversary, *mia madre!*"

Margaret and Chloe laugh. Smith says nothing but makes a strained, closed-mouth smile.

Prime adversary, he thinks, *is putting it mildly.*

"I'm really sorry, Uncle John," the girl adds, "I know being here isn't going to be easy for you."

Smith wonders, as he has so many times over the years, *What did Seraphim ever do to deserve this lovely child?*

"There's someone I want you to meet," Chloe continues, "someone you'll really like, someone who, I just know, will make this trip worthwhile for you."

A muffled grunt escapes him. *A championship Donald Ross golf course would make this trip worthwhile. There are quite a few in Canada,* he reflects, *but probably not around here.*

"And who," he asks her, like the doting uncle he is, "might that be?"

"His name is Chris Trevelyan," she tells him. "His grandfather was the original owner of Paradise Lake and miles around it, its first non-native owner, that is."

Smith tries to be polite. "What does he do?"

"He's a mostly retired RCMP officer. And yes, sometimes he wears the whole getup: red jacket, Sam Brown belt, polished brown field boots, complete with one of those Sergeant Preston of the Yukon hats." She grins.

Great, thinks Smith. He pictures the man as the cartoon character *Dudley Do-Right* and immediately becomes indignant. *I suppose that leaves me in the role of Bullwinkle. Or worse, the squirrel!*

In a natural progression, he imagines Seraphim as a combination of Boris AND Natasha. He snorts out a laugh, which he believes he has cleverly disguised as a hearty throat clearing.

"Chris still works for the RCMP as a special consultant," Chloe is telling him. "He's a great friend of the First Nation tribes, especially the Algonquin.

"He's kind of a Renaissance man," she adds. "He has a degree in neuroscience from the University of Ottawa and a law degree—from Harvard, I think. He helps the First Nation tribes in government lawsuits. When he was young, he risked his career doing it. Now the RCMP has learned to use him to their advantage to smooth out disputes before they get to court. He's their silver-haired golden boy."

So, thinks Smith, *a liberal lawyer who helps Indians.* He coughs to hide a different reaction this time, but Margaret eyes him knowingly. He can never get anything past her.

She turns to her niece. "I'm sure J.P. would love to meet Uncle Chris, Chloe."

Looking at her husband, she explains, "We call him Uncle Chris because he's always felt like one of the family."

Oh, wonderful. We're related. He frowns in the direction

of the lake.

"Why don't you take Uncle John over to meet Chris right now, Chloe?" his wife urges. "I'll finish unpacking and freshen up."

Smith pinches the bridge of his nose. He has zero interest in meeting this guy, but there's no point arguing. He is going to need every bit of Margaret's help to get through this so-called holiday.

Chloe and Smith take a leisurely walk around the lake before the road gradually peters out in front of a time-darkened log cabin. As Chloe lifts her hand to knock on the door, it opens and Smith's eyes rise.

Uncle Chris is tall, with a surprisingly abundant head of salt and pepper hair. *Mostly salt,* Smith observes, admiring the bushy but neatly trimmed white mustache.

What is he, he wonders, *six-five, six-eight?*

Chris removes an unlit briar pipe from his mouth and with obvious pleasure says, "Well, Chloe! I'm happy to see you." His bright blue eyes crinkle. "And you've brought me a guest."

She hugs him affectionately. "Uncle Chris, this is Aunt Margaret's husband, my Uncle John. It's his first visit to the lake."

"Good to meet you, John. Dame Georgina has told me about you."

Smith's jaw drops. *How the Frakk does he know her?*

His thoughts race in confusion as he follows them into the kitchen. *Dame Georgina is one of the most sought-after business consultants in the world. The woman virtually single-handedly saved my company!*

He eyes the older man appraisingly. *I want to know more*

about this guy.

Chris suggests that they sit down at a round oak table.

"Uncle Chris is helping me with my science fair project on Ayurveda," Chloe says excitedly. "It's a traditional system of medicine from India."

"What kind of project is it?" Smith asks.

"I'm trying to assess Ayurveda individual mind/body types using a new electronic pulse device that Uncle Chris and I invented."

Surprise registers on his face. "I'm impressed, Chloe. I had no idea that you were into this stuff." He looks at their host across the table. "Your Uncle Chris must be a fine mentor."

"I'll show you," she says eagerly, turning to take a small box down from the bookshelf behind her. Opening it, she takes out something that looks like an Apple watch.

"I'm going to put this on your right hand," she informs him, and proceeds to do that.

He asks, "Does it work like a Fitbit?"

"It's similar, but this baby has sensors that measure your pulse in three specific locations along the radial artery," she tells him.

"Now what?"

She pushes a tiny button on the side of the watch-like face and smiles. "Now we wait for my mom to arrive."

"Seraphim?" Smith jerks his hand back in alarm, overwhelmed by a vision of a flame-haired witch riding on the back of a ferocious fire breathing dragon. The image gets even weirder and more threatening when a piercingly loud, high-pitched beeping emanates from his wrist.

Reaching over, Chloe presses the button. The sound stops and the image disappears.

"Sorry about that," she says apologetically. "Mom isn't really coming, Uncle John. I just wanted to test the device."

She looks at Chris. "Now we know for sure that it works!"

Smith stares at her, "That was your test? Pretending that I was in imminent danger to see how I'd react? Not that I mean to refer to your mother as 'imminent danger.' "

"It's perfectly okay," she smiles sweetly. "Believe me, I know how capable she is of being exactly that," she laughs—"imminent danger. Especially to you! Which is what made it such a good test."

Chris bites into the mouthpiece of his still empty pipe. "Chloe, why don't you tell your uncle how the device works?"

She explains enthusiastically, "It measures your three main pulse rhythms and makes a different sound whenever one of them goes out of balance."

"So," says Smith, "which one of mine went out of balance?"

"That distinctive sound you heard indicates that your P Energy State was overactive and out of balance. I think you already know that a P Energy State person can quickly go out of balance when presented with a perceived threat."

He nods slowly. Dame Georgina had told him about the three main Energy States, and when he had taken the Energy State Quiz, he discovered that he was a P Energy State person, driven by a sense of purpose and a need to get things done, and subject to anger whenever he became imbalanced.

So maybe, Smith thinks defensively, *I overreact and get angry occasionally. Show me the businessperson who doesn't, especially when confronted by a ruthless rival.*

Chris looks at him from under his white brows. "I hope we didn't offend you in any way."

Chloe squeezes his hand and says, "It was for science, Uncle John. You understand."

"Don't worry," he ruffles her hair, "I understand."

He is already crunching numbers in his head as he turns to Chris. "Have you given any thought to marketing the device? With a few tweaks, it might have a chance to beat out Apple and Fitbit."

He pauses. "Turn it back on. Let's see what my pulse says now."

This time it's Chris who presses the ON button, but there's no beeping, no sound at all.

"Your pulse is perfectly normal again," Chloe tells him. "You recover fast!"

Smith waggles his eyebrows in a goofy Groucho Marx imitation. "It's one of my specialties."

PROLOGUE COMMENTARY

Energy States

The principle of Energy States is derived from Ayurveda, India's comprehensive and prevention-oriented system of natural medicine which addresses our body, mind, and environment. This holistic approach to health evaluates each person according to his or her *"dosha,"* the individual mind/body type or nature, which we refer to in this book as an Energy State. There are three fundamental Energy States that are traditionally called Vata, Pitta, and Kapha.

We use the letter V to represent Vata, P to represent Pitta, and K to represent Kapha. Each of these Energy States, V, P, and K, can occur singly or in combination of any two or even all three. [Note to Reader: In *Gut Crisis* and *The Rest And Repair Diet*, we use the expression Gut/Brain Nature rather than Energy State to refer to the individual mind/body type. And in *Beauty, Ayurveda, and Essential Oil Skincare* we call it the Brain/Body Nature or type. The terms differentiate slightly according to the focus of the book, but they all refer to Vata, Pitta, and Kapha, and are virtually interchangeable.]

Ayurveda has long possessed the ability to precisely determine how different factors influence each Energy State, either positively or negatively. Diet, for example, is an important factor, which creates either balance or imbalance in our Energy State. We all react differently to environmental triggers, and while modern science has only recently discovered that different foods turn genes on or off, Ayurveda has understood the far-reaching effect of food for centuries. Epigenetic is the term given to the study of how environmental factors affect the DNA without changing its basic structure, and some researchers consider Ayurveda to be an ancient science of epigenetics. Research supports the scientific basis of Ayurveda, showing significant correlation between the three main Energy States (doshas) and specific genetic and physiological measures. There is even a new field called Ayurgenomics devoted to this research. For more information, go to Resource Materials Section 1.

Ayurveda identifies specific environmental triggers that cause people to go out of balance and perform poorly. By understanding your Energy State, it is much easier for you to adopt and maintain positive new habits.

You can determine your personal Energy State through an examination by a trained Ayurveda expert, or by taking the simple Quiz below, adapted from *The Coherence Code*. More detailed versions can be found at docgut.com, doshaguru.com, and dharmaparenting.com.

Energy State Quiz

V ENERGY STATE	STRONGLY DISAGREE / STRONGLY AGREE
1. Light sleeper, difficulty falling asleep	[1] [2] [3] [4] [5]
2. Irregular appetite	[1] [2] [3] [4] [5]
3. Learns quickly but forgets quickly	[1] [2] [3] [4] [5]
4. Easily becomes overstimulated	[1] [2] [3] [4] [5]
5. Does not tolerate cold weather very well	[1] [2] [3] [4] [5]
6. A sprinter rather than a marathoner	[1] [2] [3] [4] [5]
7. Speech is energetic, with frequent changes in topic	[1] [2] [3] [4] [5]
8. Anxious and worried when under stress	[1] [2] [3] [4] [5]
V SCORE	(TOTAL YOUR RESPONSES)

P Energy State	*Strongly Disagree / Strongly Agree*
1. Easily becomes overheated	[1] [2] [3] [4] [5]
2. Strong reaction when challenged	[1] [2] [3] [4] [5]
3. Uncomfortable when meals are delayed	[1] [2] [3] [4] [5]
4. Good at physical activity	[1] [2] [3] [4] [5]
5. Strong appetite	[1] [2] [3] [4] [5]
6. Good sleeper but may not need as much sleep as others	[1] [2] [3] [4] [5]
7. Clear and precise speech	[1] [2] [3] [4] [5]
8. Becomes irritable and/or angry under stress	[1] [2] [3] [4] [5]
P Score	*(Total your responses)*

K ENERGY STATE	STRONGLY DISAGREE / STRONGLY AGREE
1. Slow eater	[1] [2] [3] [4] [5]
2. Falls asleep easily but wakes up slowly	[1] [2] [3] [4] [5]
3. Steady, stable temperament	[1] [2] [3] [4] [5]
4. Doesn't mind waiting to eat	[1] [2] [3] [4] [5]
5. Slow to learn but rarely forgets	[1] [2] [3] [4] [5]
6. Good physical strength and stamina	[1] [2] [3] [4] [5]
7. Speech may be slow and thoughtful	[1] [2] [3] [4] [5]
8. Possessive and stubborn under stress	[1] [2] [3] [4] [5]
K SCORE	(TOTAL YOUR RESPONSES)

Compare all three scores. Whichever total is higher, V, P, or K, is your primary Energy State. It is common to have two high scores and one lower score. This indicates that you are a combination of two main Energy States, with a minor influence from the third. In some cases, you may have three similar scores. This is somewhat rare and indicates that you are a Tri-Energy State. You may also find that your score highlights only one Energy State. This means that every aspect of your life is strongly influenced by this Energy State.

CHAPTER 1

Tippy Canoe

Early the next morning Chloe comes over to visit J.P. and Margaret. "I feel bad about surprising you yesterday," she tells her uncle. "I'd like to make it up to you, and it's so pretty out today that Uncle Chris offered to take us for a canoe ride."

"Oh, yes, John," Margaret exclaims enthusiastically. "I'd love you to go out on the lake, it's such a special part of my childhood."

Smith puts on a happy face. "Sounds great."

I have to do it for Margaret's sake, he thinks, *even though the last thing I want to do is go out on the lake in some tippy canoe.*

"But Chloe dear," her aunt says, "we were going to plan your mother's birthday party today. Let John and Uncle Chris go together, it will give them a chance to get to know each other."

Chloe looks at him inquiringly.

He shrugs and says, "No problem." *I suppose a little canoe ride is no big deal,* he tells himself, *and I'm curious about Chris.*

"I'll see you later," he says, waving to the ladies.

He strides down the dirt road, breathing in the cool clean Canadian air. The newly minted morning sky is insanely blue and there seem to be more birds singing than he has ever heard before.

The sun feels hot on his shoulders by the time Smith reaches Chris's cabin. Looking in the window, Smith is utterly shocked to see Chris sitting on the floor in full lotus position. More accurately, Smith realizes, he only sits for a few seconds before his whole body appears to lift up, inches above the floor, and almost, almost—hovers for a couple of seconds before landing. It happens again! And again! *What the freaking Frakk?*

Smith is open-mouthed as a beached carp. Smacking his hand on his forehead, he wonders, *Did I drink too much wine with dinner last night? Did Margaret slip hallucinogens into my breakfast juice? I mean, what the freaking Frakk?*

With extreme diffidence this time, he again peers into the window. The room is empty. He looks around, wondering what he should do.

As he decides to knock on the door, it opens. There's Chris in front of him. *Looking completely normal.*

"Good morning!" the man exclaims with great cheer.

Smith swallows. "Good morning. I-I-I happened to see you in there..." his voice trails off.

Chris smiles broadly. "And you want to know what I was doing, right?"

"Uh-huh," is all Smith can manage in response.

"I was just finishing my morning meditation. It picks this old body right up!"

Picks it up is right! thinks Smith, but he does not comment. *Maybe I didn't see what I think I saw. Maybe it's me.*

Maybe I'm muzzy-headed from travel, or all this fresh piney air is getting to me.

He has just decided to dismiss the experience and pretend that it never happened, when the welcome aroma of strong, freshly brewed coffee embraces his sense of smell. Like iron filings to a magnet, he is drawn into the kitchen where Chris is already pouring out a steaming mug for each of them.

"Isn't Chloe joining us for our canoe ride?" he asks.

"Oh, she's busy with Margaret getting ready for Seraphim's party," says Smith.

"Of course, I forgot about that."

After drinking their coffee in companionable silence, they leave the cabin and head down to the water. When they reach the edge of the steep hill directly above the lake, Smith sees slabs of hewn granite set into the earth all the way down, apparently serving as sharp-edged steps. A weathered dock extends out into the water below, and at the far end, a beautiful cedar canoe is tied bow and stern to iron cleats.

Smith's footsteps echo on worn gray wood as he walks past a tackle case and fishing rods. Admiring the finely worked honey-colored canoe with its hand-woven cane seats, he remarks, "She's a beauty."

"It was made by a First Nation woodworker friend of mine," Chris tells him. "Not a day goes by that I don't admire his craftsmanship."

"I thought they went in for birchbark canoes?"

"Oh, they make them too," Chris chuckles, digging into

a waterproof bag he has brought with him and drawing out a couple of life preservers.

"Oh, I don't think I need that," Smith says. "I'm a strong swimmer."

"So am I," Chris replies quietly, "and I think that you do."

Smith stares as he squats to free the canoe from its mooring.

If anyone else challenged me like that, thinks Smith, *I'd be furious. But,* he scratches his chin, perplexed, *the only thing I feel,* he realizes, *is interested in this guy.*

"I'll climb in first," Chis tells him, stepping easily into the canoe, "and keep it still for you."

He sits on the stern seat and holds the boat close to the dock. "You can get in now, John. Grab the gunnels as you step down."

"Gunnels?" Smith repeats.

"Yeah, spelled gunwales," Chris says. "Put your hands on either side to help you balance."

Smith eyes the vessel. For some reason, it suddenly looks awfully far down. He tries not to show concern, but as he extends a foot towards the ribbed flooring, he feels very unstable.

Chris grips his arm firmly, helping him in. Smith is making his way to the bow seat as Chris says, "She's a little tippy but she's the fastest canoe on Paradise Lake."

Aren't I the lucky one, thinks Smith sarcastically, praying that he won't make a fool of himself and tip the thing over.

When he is safely seated, Chris slides one of two handmade maple paddles from under the seats and uses it to propel the canoe out on the lake.

Smith's nervousness vanishes as he witnesses Chris's obvious skill. Each stroke of his paddle cuts the water cleanly, propelling them effortlessly forward. The surface of the lake is like a reflecting glass. On one side wild ducks swim peacefully and somewhere a loon cries. From the middle of the lake, Smith can see the Laurentian mountains. He looks around—there's no direction that isn't beautiful. *No wonder it's called Paradise Lake.*

The men don't talk as they move across the lake, which is thickly bordered with tall evergreens. Occasionally a house appears, tucked between the trees. Smith is enjoying himself.

"Would you like to paddle?" offers Chris.

"I don't know how to manage a canoe," Smith admits reluctantly.

"There's nothing easier. I'm happy to teach you."

Smith's pleasant, carefree moment becomes slightly shadowed with anxiety.

"Don't worry," Chris says jovially, "it's easier than golf!"

"Hah!" exclaims Smith. "Everything is easier than golf!"

Chris holds the second paddle out to Smith. "Grasp it with one hand about a foot and a half or so down the shaft," he instructs, "and at the top with your other hand. Start with your paddle almost vertical, about ninety degrees, then as you pull it back, angle it to about forty-five degrees with the face of the paddle against the water. Try not to dip it into the water too deeply."

Smith makes some awkward practice strokes. At first he is too tentative and the resistance of the water causes his paddle to wobble weirdly.

"Keep practicing," Chris tells him. "You're doing fine. I only have one persnickety rule about paddling."

"What's that?"

"Never let the paddle scrape the side of the canoe when you draw it back. Bring it as close as you can without actually touching the side. This will take time to master, so for now, allow yourself some leeway. But don't strain."

Sure, don't scrape but don't strain. Easy to say, harder to do! He attempts a stroke which moves the boat forward, but as he draws the paddle back it clunks horribly against the side of the canoe.

"Never mind, never mind," Chris reassures him. "Give yourself a bigger safety margin, five or six inches. As in golf, finesse comes with practice."

This is harder than it looks, Smith realizes.

"Don't be too tough on yourself. What you're doing now is like picking up a club for the first time and trying to hit the ball. There are a few fundamentals to master before you get fancy. It won't be long before you are paddling a canoe as naturally as you make a Quantum golf swing."

"What??" Smith exclaims, twisting quickly around on his seat and causing the canoe to lurch precipitously to the side. His heartbeat skyrockets. But Chris continues to paddle as if nothing happened.

Realizing that they are not about to capsize, Smith starts to breathe normally again, and tentatively resumes paddling.

"How do you know about the Q swing?" he asks.

"I learned it from Linc."

Smith stops paddling and peers at Chris over his shoulder. "How did you meet him?"

"Dame Georgina and Linc and I were at Camp David together some years ago."

Camp David! What the Frakk were they doing at the famous presidential retreat?

Chris doesn't elaborate, so Smith decides not to pursue it and applies himself to his paddle strokes with renewed vigor and determination. The canoe cuts through the water.

"I love being here," he admits quietly. "Margaret has talked about it for years."

"She's a wonderful person," Chris comments.

"I know," says Smith simply. "Margaret's the best part of my life. Being up here gives me a greater appreciation of who she is. I don't know why, but I feel surprisingly peaceful right now. I mean, I get that I'm not perfect and there are a lot of things that I need to improve."

"Like what?"

Smith speaks about personal details of his life as if the two of them have known each other for years.

"And Margaret's been concerned about my health lately," he discloses. "You can probably tell that I don't exercise enough. I play a lot of golf, but I'm not thrilled about dragging a bag of clubs around for eighteen holes, so I pretty much always ride in a cart."

He glances ruefully at his belly. "I'm afraid I'm losing my personal Battle of the Bulge."

"Your wife is a wise woman, John. Life isn't very good

without health."

"I know it. But these days every doctor, fitness instructor, and his uncle, seem to be hawking a weight loss program on TV or the internet. They're all in it for money, and it makes me want to run in the opposite direction."

"I can understand," Chris empathizes.

A few minutes later, he suggests that Smith try paddling on the other side of the canoe. And he changes the subject.

"Do you remember Linc talking about the importance of having your attention on the whole of your golf swing rather than the parts?"

"Yeah, I liked that. But what does it have to do with my weight problem?" He goes on without waiting for Chris to respond, "I wouldn't want you to take this the wrong way, Chris, but I'd rather you don't use any dang physics principles. Linc does that sometimes and it goes right over my head."

Because he is facing forward, Smith can't see Chris smile.

"No physics," the older man agrees. "I just want to point out that in order to resolve certain problems, and a weight problem is a good example, you have to consider deeper aspects of your life. If you focus on the parts and disregard the whole, it will be almost impossible to find a long-lasting solution. Most weight loss programs don't work because they don't deal with the underlying causes."

Smith is interested in spite of himself. "What should I do first?"

"Good question."

After a couple of perfect paddle strokes, he asks, "What is the main purpose of your life, John?"

Smith lays his paddle across his knees, keeping a good grip on it. "I suppose my main purpose is to be a successful businessman so I can provide for my family and contribute to my community."

"Good. This is an indication that you have some sense of the whole of life. Do you happen to remember what Dame Georgina called 'the path of life?' "

"Ha! You mean dharma," Smith says, pleased to know the answer.

"That's right," agrees Chris. "And the word dharma has several meanings. For now, let's consider it as the path of life. When your Energy State is in good balance, that is when you are most able to live your dharma, the path of life which most supports you. Understanding your own Energy State is understanding yourself. You are aware that you are a P Energy State person, right?"

"Right." Smith dips his paddle into the water, pulling a short powerful stroke. "That's what the Quiz said, and it's what I've been told."

He feels that he is starting to get the hang of twisting the face of the paddle at the end of each stroke.

"I'm a fiery guy," he goes on. "And between you and me, I kinda like that image, except, of course, that it means I get mad too easily. Anyway, how does understanding my Energy State help me lose weight?"

"Weight loss isn't an easy habit to change. But being willing to look at the whole of your life can help you to go beyond the immediate problem, so that you can start to deal with its causes."

"How do the Frakk do I do that?"

"How the Frakk indeed," laughs Chris.

He goes on more seriously, "You need a perspective which includes understanding who you are, how you see the world, and your path in it."

"In business," Smith tells him, "what you're describing is like changing the entire strategic plan of a company to solve a simple production problem."

"That is an astute observation," Chris comments.

Smith makes another strong paddle stroke and forgets to turn the face of the paddle at the end. It would have drawn them off course, except that Chris compensates by calmly twisting his own paddle, redirecting them steadily forward.

"Internal problems in a business," he tells Smith, "are often the result of a fearful and disorderly company culture or mindset. We can try to solve individual problems in such an environment, but it's like putting out an endless series of fires. It is far more effective to introduce a healthier mindset, one which is based on mutual trust and psychological safety. Problems can then be solved much more easily, and often due to the initiative of the employees themselves."

"That's what Dame Georgina was talking about!"

"Yes," Chris tells him, "and the same principles can be applied to your personal life. When you take a look at the whole of your life—your childhood experiences, your life plan, your dharma—a larger picture becomes clear. Habit change is much more effective when you understand the underlying causes of the habit you are trying to change."

"Let's say for the sake of argument," Smith proposes, "that I agree with you and I'm interested. What do I do next?"

"You've already taken the first step. You have expressed Receptivity and a desire to grow."

He pauses. "Remember the Coherence Code that Dame Georgina taught you?"

"How could I forget? It's what saved my company."

"What I'm going to suggest," continues Chris, "is similar, but it applies to your personal life.

"Let's talk about your Energy State. Do you know why it's important for you to know your own Energy State when it comes to changing habits?"

"As I understand it, every Energy State type approaches change differently. P Energy State people, like me, are generally goal-oriented and we have good discipline, so it's easier for us to change a habit. I think Georgina said that most habit change books are written by P Energy State people for P Energy State people!"

"That's true. P Energy State people find it relatively easy to create a plan and stick to it. When they are out of balance, though, it isn't any easier for them to make a positive change than it is for a V or a K Energy State person."

"Why?"

"Because the unbalanced P Energy State individual becomes

impatient and frustrated and gets angry at what or who they are dealing with, and at anyone else who happens to be nearby."

"Yeah, yeah, I know," Smith has to admit. "But I remember the other two main types also have problems when they go out of balance."

"Ex-actly," Chris says, slapping the surface of the water with the flat of his paddle for emphasis. "V Energy State people excel in imagination and creativity, but they have difficulty staying focused when they are unbalanced.

"I'm sure you know that many of our worst habits are due to old psychological trauma, and since V Energy State people are very sensitive, they are basically ruled by their inner emotions. When V Energy State people go out of balance," he explains, "they get nervous or anxious, maybe fearful. Even physiologically, they tend to be more delicately built and they are usually thin when they are young. If their Energy State is continually out of balance, which often happens when they age, they can become overweight. And a V Energy person often consumes carbs as a way of dealing with emotional problems."

"Doesn't everyone?"

"Yes, of course," Chris agrees, "many people do that. V Energy State folks to do it to a greater extent."

"I thought that K Energy State people were the most likely to be overweight?"

"True. They tend to love food and their slower metabolism causes them to gain weight easily."

"Georgina taught my company," recalls Smith, "to encourage

our K Energy State people to spend some time exercising every day, and we made sure that our P Energy State employees and managers ate on time, which helped them control their volatile tempers. We had the V Energy State people sipping hot water or tea with Vata balancing herbs throughout the day to keep them more grounded. And one weekend a month we organized fun activities that were specifically suited to each Energy State type. Everyone reported that they were communicating better and had more energy. It was great!

"But what does all of this have to do with my extra weight?"

Chris explains, "The point is that you don't have to be a K Energy State person to be overweight. It can happen to anyone. You, for instance."

Smith carefully turns his head so that he can look briefly at his mentor.

"You haven't really put much attention on losing weight, have you?" Chris asks sympathetically.

Smith shrugs. "Not really."

"Do you think you could lose weight if you watched your calories?"

"Maybe. I don't think it would be very hard for me to cut back if I put my mind to it. But I enjoy apple pie and ice cream." He laughs. "And to tell you the truth, I don't really mind having a pot belly."

"You are a very accomplished person," Chris tells him, "and you've already learned a lot from two extraordinary teachers. What I'm going to suggest to you now is a small addition to your life."

Smith enjoys the opening compliment, though he's pretty sure it is going to be followed by something he won't enjoy.

"Obviously," Chris says, "there are still a few challenges in your life."

"Such as?"

"Such as your relationship with Seraphim."

Smith's spirits deflate. *Why the Frakk does he have to bring her up in the middle of our conversation?*

The sound of a powerful motor draws their attention and they turn to see a rapidly approaching speedboat. A beautiful old Chris Craft is moving towards them at an alarming speed.

"Paddle hard!" yells Chris. "We have to get to shore before she swamps us."

Smith doesn't have to be told twice. They dig their paddles into the water and the canoe surges forward.

Smith cries breathlessly, "Who's this 'she' you're talking about?"

"Your nemesis," replies Chris grimly.

Smith knows exactly who he means. *My Frakking sister-in-law has haunted me for years, now she's ruining my experience at this beautiful lake.*

When the canoe crunches onto the sandy shore, he is thrown violently forward moments before the powerboat roars by and an enormous wake deluges their boat, filling it with water. Both men are soaked.

Almost in wonder, Smith says, "She's crazy."

"She's probably having a Pitta attack," Chris tells him, water dripping from his white brows. "What did you do to her to make her so angry?"

Wait a minute, thinks Smith. *Is he saying that this is my fault?*

TROUBLE IN PARADISE

CHAPTER 1 COMMENTARY

TBC Life Coaching

This book focuses on the application of Total Brain Coaching or TBC to your personal life and in Chapter One, we see Chris helping Smith take the first step towards improving his relationship with Seraphim. He has already used TBC successfully in his company; now he learns about the 7 Steps of TBC Life Coaching in his personal life:

1. Discover Yourself
2. Habit Map and Plan
3. Attention
4. Rhythm
5. Maintain Balance
6. Integrate and Improve
7. Celebrate

Chris acknowledges that Smith has discovered a great deal about himself from two great teachers. In *Quantum Golf*, Smith met

Linc St. Claire, an extraordinary golf instructor and spiritual guide, who showed him how to swing a golf club and be momentarily in tune with the cosmos. In *The Coherence Code,* he met Dame Georgina St. George, a world-class business consultant and coach, whose system of Total Brain Coaching took Smith's company from the brink of failure to success. To see how each of these 7 Steps relate to the seven principles in the book *Total Brain Coaching* see Final Commentary: Applying Total Brain Coaching to Your Life.

In order to discover more about himself Smith must be receptive to change, willing to learn. In business, this is called having a growth mindset rather than a fixed mindset, and it can begin as simply as being open to new ideas. Once you are receptive, your next step is finding a teacher, coach, or partner, who will help you. If you can't find the right person, then you look for knowledge that can help you.

It would be wonderful if all parents were also great coaches, but unfortunately, this is rarely the case. If you are lucky, you might have a couple of good teachers in school, or maybe one good coach who really cares. Often you don't find a great teacher until later in life, and in many cases your partner or spouse becomes your life coach, acting as a "mirror" and cheerleader to help you gain a broader perspective on life.

Some find a mentor, psychological counselor, or a spiritual guide. If you are very fortunate, the person you find may be a master of both material and spiritual life. Some of the greatest teachers in the world are no longer living, but their teachings can be accessed in books and on video.

Western philosophy considers Socrates to be one of the ultimate teachers. We mention him particularly because he created what is known as the Socratic method, asking questions in order to unfold deep inner knowledge. A TBC life coach uses questions to help clients learn more about themselves and to enable them to make their own decisions: Asking rather than telling.

The greatest spiritual traditions and religions, Eastern and Western, have been inspired by teachers who have been considered to be masters, saints, or even divine beings. However great your teacher may be, what you learn from them depends on your receptivity and commitment.

For most of his life, Smith has naturally had fairly clear goals. In *The Coherence Code*, we witness his intention to be a successful businessman. In *Quantum Golf*, his main goal is to become a better golfer. Throughout both books, and also in our most recent book, *Beauty, Ayurveda, and Essential Oil Skincare—A Friendly Introduction*, currently in press, Smith wants a healthy, happy, and fulfilled family life, and we see that he loves and respects his wife, and acknowledges her intuition and intelligence. His main weakness, his greatest flaw, and his worst habit, is his tendency to lose his temper. This is especially evident in his relationship with his sister-in-law Seraphim.

CHAPTER 2

The Black Hole of Calcutta

Smith stares morosely out at the lake, absentmindedly washing a large bunch of freshly picked spinach under the cold water tap. He is feeling burdened by the general unfairness of life, specifically with Margaret's having invited Seraphim to dinner.

He decides to voice his objection one last time. "I fail to see why we should feed her after she practically drowned me."

Patiently, Margaret replies, "I told you, John. We're finally all together at Paradise Lake and we're going to sit down in peace and have a nice family meal."

There is a two-second pause before she goes on, "Besides, it might not have been you that she was after."

He looks at her, allowing the water to wash the spinach by itself. "What do you mean? Why on earth is she mad at him?"

"Because Chris has a painting that Seraphim desperately wants. He won it by outbidding her in an estate auction. So not only does she covet the artwork, her pride is damaged. And when he got the painting professionally cleaned and evaluated, it turned out to be a long-lost landscape by a famous early Canadian painter. It's very valuable."

She sighs. "I don't think she will ever forgive him."

"If that's the case, maybe we got off lucky!"

"Maybe you did. Anyway, I want this meal to be a healing celebration."

Ah boy, he thinks, *that's it then. Margaret has taken the high road and her mind is made up.* They have been married long enough for him to know that there's no use arguing further. He shakes his head.

Lifting up the large strainer, which is filled to the brim with wet spinach, he joggles it fiercely up and down to drain off the water. *Here I am, cleaning spinach for a witch. Spelled with a Frakking "B"!*

Plopping the damp leaves into a large wooden bowl, he swipes his hands on his chinos and leaves the kitchen. Like the good husband he tries to be when he remembers, he proceeds to set the table in the glass-enclosed room overlooking the lake.

His mouth waters at the aroma of two organic chickens roasting in the oven and a fig sauce simmering on the stovetop.

Margaret opens the door for Chloe and her mother, who walks into the cottage as if she owns it, which she once did. Chloe goes into the kitchen to help her aunt.

Unnoticed and wanting to stay that way, Smith slips into a small bedroom down the hall to lay low until it's time to eat. He stretches out on the bed and waits impatiently, and it's not long before he hears Margaret call from the dining room, "Dinner is served."

The moment he walks in, he sees that his sacred place at the head of the table has been usurped by his red-headed nemesis. Barely containing his indignation and annoyance, he seats himself down in the only empty chair, which happens to be right beside Seraphim.

"How was your first experience with canoeing, Uncle John?" Chloe asks with innocent expectation.

Smith's face is a smiling mask as he replies, "Ah, it was a cuppa tea, bowl o'cherries, piece a'cake!"

"Shall we have the spinach salad first?" Margaret suggests, serving each plate generously.

"What did you put in the dressing, Aunt Margaret?" asks Chloe. "It's fabulous."

"Oh, a little of this and little of that. I'll email you the recipe."

"Tasty, Margaret," Smith nods, enjoying the fresh greens.

"Delicious," Seraphim exclaims, filling her mouth with a heaping forkful and chewing vigorously.

Almost immediately, there is an audible crack! Seraphim shrieks and her hand flies to her mouth…when she takes it away, she spits out a front tooth.

"Oh no," Margaret cries, "the spinach must not have been cleaned thoroughly!"

He swallows uncomfortably. *I really tried to clean it well,* he thinks, genuinely feeling badly for his sister-in-law. His compassion withers and fades when she gives him one of her infamous death glares.

With that front tooth missing, he thinks meanly, *she looks like an old hillbilly.* As the theme from the movie *Deliverance* plays in his head, he covers his mouth with his hand to hide what he knows is a horribly inappropriate smile.

Narrowing her eyes to slits, Seraphim leans over to him so that only he can hear. "You thould know, brother-in-law," she lisps, giving him a hideous gap-toothed grin and poking her fleshy pink tongue through the cavity, "you have let looth the hounds of war!"

Standing abruptly, she knocks her chair down behind her and strides heavily out of the house. Chloe flutters behind.

"Oh, John," Margaret moans, "what have you done?"

That night Smith sleeps fitfully. Just before dawn, he puts his clothes on and tiptoes out to see Chris.

His feet crunch satisfyingly on the stony road…*A peaceful canoe ride might be calming*, he thinks. *But I've raised the ante for revenge, and I doubt that it will be safe on the lake.*

It's not as if he intentionally harmed his sister-in-law. He had washed the spinach to the best of his ability. He'd been a little distracted, but he had done an adequate job.

It must have been fate, he concludes, *that made me miss the one tiny stone destined to crack her tooth*. The mental image of her cavernous oral gap is accompanied by an ominous expression—*The Black Hole of Calcutta!*

CHAPTER 2 COMMENTARY

Karma

This chapter deals with the inevitable and unfathomable nature of karma. The basic truth about karma is that all action has a reaction. Science demonstrates this understanding in Newton's third law: For every action, there is an equal and opposite reaction. And most of us are familiar with the Biblical saying, "As you sow, so shall you reap."

Smith attributes Seraphim's mishap to bad luck, but no one has any idea of what actions may have transpired between these protagonists in another life.

TROUBLE IN PARADISE

CHAPTER 3

Fatigue is the Enemy

When Smith reaches Chris's cabin, he looks in the window to make sure that Chris is up, and sees him.

Yep, there he is, sitting at the table having breakfast, instead of hovering off the ground. What was that about anyway?

He knocks at the door and Chris quickly opens it. Smith walks in. With one hand Chris motions for Smith to sit down, and with the other, slides a plate of freshly baked scones across the table.

"Coffee?" he asks, already filling a large mug for his guest.

"Oh yeah," Smith says gratefully. After several steaming gulps, he recounts the dinner disaster.

Chris listens, but he doesn't go into the details of Smith's mishap. He makes non-committal but sympathetic comments like, "I see," and "I understand."

And when Smith falls quiet, he offers to take him canoeing. "The early morning air will help take your mind off your troubles. But it might be wise for us to stay close to shore," he warns, "even though Seraphim is unlikely to be awake at this hour."

Out on the lake, the rising sun reflects gold in the still water and Smith feels relief flooding through him.

"Have you given any thought to what I said yesterday?" Chris asks, paddling quietly in the stern.

"I'm afraid I've had other things on my mind," Smith replies, straining a little to prevent his paddle from scraping the side of the canoe.

"Sure, that's understandable. We were talking about dharma and the path of life, and I suggested that in order to change a habit, you must first consider its relationship to the deeper whole of your life. It's part of discovering who you are."

Smith frowns a little. *I don't remember that,* he thinks, but makes a vaguely affirmative sound anyway.

"The reality is that you have been making discoveries about yourself for a very long time," Chris tells him.

"I have?"

"Of course you have. One of most important parts of discovering yourself is finding and learning from a great teacher. You found two, Linc and Dame Georgina, and you've learned a lot from them. They both gave you a clearer vision of who you are and what you want to become. They also helped you change yourself by changing your habits."

"Yeah." Smith scratches his forehead. "I guess so."

"And do you remember the tools that Dame Georgina gave you?"

"You mean the Total Brain Coaching tools?" asks Smith.

"Exactly."

"Sure, I also remember," he boasts a little, "that the word DHARMIC is an acronym for each of the tools."

"That's very good," Chris compliments him.

Smith is glad that he is facing forward so Chris can't tell that he is blushing with pleasure.

"Okay," continues Chris, "let's review the first tool. In TBC Life Coaching the letter D in DHARMIC stands for: Discover Yourself."

Smith interrupts. "If there's one thing I know about myself, thanks to TBC, it's that I'm a P Energy State person. So, as we said yesterday, it shouldn't be incredibly hard for me to alter my bad habits. I've always known that I have a strong will and I'm good at making changes."

"Again, you're exactly right. And after you have discovered your individual Energy State, one of the best ways to begin to change your habits is to create a Habit Map and a Habit Plan, both of which relate to the H in DHARMIC."

They paddle without speaking for a while, then Chris suggests that they talk about what remaining habits are important for Smith.

Thinking for a moment, Smith asks, "Such as?"

"Such as getting along with difficult people."

Smith carefully turns to look at him. "Like Seraphim, you mean?"

"Oh, yes, that's who I mean," Chris says, his voice rising and falling almost musically.

Smith's brow furrows like an accordion. "You do realize that getting along with Seraphim is like climbing Mount Everest blindfolded. And backwards."

Chris chuckles. "You're right."

Smith lays his paddle across the gunnels in front of him. "Look, all of this is fine and dandy, but because of my 'karma' or whatever, I still have gigantic problems with Seraphim. Probably worse now than before."

Chris doesn't make a comment, but he asks, "Remember what I said about balance?"

"Sure. If my P Energy State goes out of balance, I get impatient and prone to anger. But what about fear? I've been feeling some of that lately."

"Fear and anxiety are almost always the result of a V Energy State imbalance, but P and K Energy State people also experience fear. Given your present circumstances, I would say that fear is a natural and even valuable response."

Smith's eyes move quickly around the perimeter of the lake to make sure that Seraphim isn't in the process of launching a sneak attack.

Chris grins. "And you remember the idea of a keystone or Super Habit?"

He twists around, even more carefully this time, to face him. "Is that a trick question? I know perfectly well that both Linc and Georgina wanted me to learn to meditate. And I know that meditation is a Super Habit that helps change other habits."

Facing the front of the canoe again, he says, "I just haven't found the time to learn."

"The world is challenging for all us," Chris acknowledges, "and meditation is extremely helpful in dealing with the stress of life. Not that you have any of that, of course."

"Very funny," retorts Smith. "I know that meditation, particularly Transcendental Meditation, has been shown to reduce heart disease and increase intelligence and creativity. You don't have to sell me on it. I get it that TM is like a silver bullet for stress."

"Okay, we can talk about your meditating another time," says Chris nonchalantly. "But tell me, what is it you do, which you believe helps to keep you in balance?"

"Besides golf?" Smith asks.

"Besides golf."

After considering for a moment, Smith says, "Thanks to Ayurveda, I learned that I absolutely need to have my meals on time, especially lunch. I also have to avoid getting overheated, like not playing golf in Palm Springs during the summer. And weird though it sounds, spicy food affects my temper. Thank goodness Margaret keeps track of what I eat, so that's one thing I don't have to worry about!"

"What about exercise and yoga?"

"What about them?" asks Smith, unaware that his tone is slightly confrontational.

"Besides golf," Chris continues patiently, "what else do you like to do?"

"I like to take long walks with Margaret in the morning and evening, and I like swimming and body surfing. I put my foot down when it comes to yoga. I have no desire to twist myself into a pretzel."

"Okay, but what if there were some yoga postures that could help improve your golf game?"

"You mean something that would help prevent my back from going out if I play too much?"

"Yes, for one thing."

"I might try it," Smith says reflectively.

Chris continues, "What about a fitness program which is specifically designed to help your golf game? Lots of pros do that today. I'm not suggesting anything too radical. I'm talking about a program that is suitable for your age and fitness."

"I'd definitely be interested."

"Good. There are certain things which each Energy State can do in order to stay in balance. But there's one thing that damages all of them."

"What's that?"

"Fatigue. Fatigue is the enemy. And you can quote me."

"Ha!" says Smith. "I thought Seraphim was the enemy."

"For you to be able to deal effectively with Seraphim, or any another antagonist, your brain cells must be firing coherently. And that means you have to get proper rest."

Smith grunts and scratches his head. "I couldn't even sleep last night just thinking about what she might do to me. Maybe I'll grab a nap this afternoon on Margaret's watch."

"That's a start."

Their canoe is gliding through the water in perfect peace towards the mouth of a beautiful water lily-filled bay, when the roar of twin 200 horsepower Evinrude motors shatters the silence.

Smith's brain circuits scream simultaneously, *Fight or Flight! Fight or Flight!* Flight appears to have the upper hand.

Chris, who is equally alert but far more stable, yells, "Paddle hard. I'll steer into the inlet where it's shallow and she can't follow us."

They are both paddling with renewed energy, determined to avoid the approaching powerboat as the engine noise grows louder and louder. They don't allow themselves time to look back until the water around them has become almost choked with flowering plants.

Allowing the canoe to move slowly forward on its own, they turn to see the speedboat race right past the outlet. The sound of the motors diminishes, fading away entirely.

"It's not Seraphim," says Chris with a big grin.

"No, but I'm glad we didn't take a chance," Smith declares. "She's so wild there's no telling what she will do next."

But I'm pretty sure that whatever it is won't be as simple as swamping our canoe!

TROUBLE IN PARADISE

CHAPTER 3 COMMENTARY

DHARMIC

In this chapter Chris reviews the first two steps: Discover Yourself and Habit Map and Plan. He then introduces Smith to the third Step: Habit Map and Plan.

Since you know that the word DHARMIC serves as an acronym that describes 7 Steps which will help you change your habits, let's look at the first two letters in the acronym.

D

The D in DHARMIC stands for: Discover Yourself. Smith has already begun this process by learning about his Energy State. You can discover your own Energy State by taking the Quiz in the Commentary in the Prologue. (If you haven't taken it yet, it will be good to do it now.)

Each of us has a different nature and individual tendencies which underlie our habits. In order to make a change in life, it is essential to understand who you really are. For more information, go to Resource Materials Section 1 to see a summary of the 3 main

Energy States and scientific research validating them.

H

The letter H in DHARMIC stands for: Habit Map and Habit Plan. In order to change a habit we need to have a clear intention of what we want to change. It will help you to begin with a Habit Map:

- In the middle of a clean piece of paper, or on your computer screen, write down what it is that you want to change as it occurs to you.

- Around this, like spokes radiating from the hub of a wheel, list specific strategies that you think will help you implement the change.

- Now prioritize your ideas and come up with a Habit Plan which identifies the one habit you want to change.

It is easier to create a new habit than to try to change an old one. The brain has an extraordinary ability called neuroplasticity, which means that it constantly changes throughout your life, forming new connections and pathways.

The pathways you use regularly are strengthened, while pathways that are not being used either disappear or become dormant—an excellent example of "Use it or lose it."

Brain development is also an example of nature vs. nurture. Your DNA is programmed to create basic pathways, but your environment affects your DNA and can change existing pathways. Every time you learn a new skill, or have a new experience, or create a new habit, your brain changes.

Think of a habit as a highway along which information flows unimpeded. The longer you have the habit, the larger and more powerful the highway becomes and the harder it is to change. Creating a new habit requires building a new pathway in your brain, which takes both time and energy.

Simple habits, however, take a relatively short time to establish, while more difficult habits take longer. One study showed that it took 20 days to establish the simple habit of drinking a glass of water at the beginning of the day, while it took 84 days to establish the habit of doing 50 sit-ups every day. See the Resource Materials in Section 5 for how TBC compares with other habit change programs.

One of the most important and revolutionary scientific discoveries of our time is the existence of the gut-brain axis and its influence on mental and physical health. It is necessary to rewire your brain in order to create a new habit, and energy is required to do this. Improving your gut health boosts your energy level and makes your entire Energy State more powerful. For more about the gut-brain axis, see Resource Materials Section 3.

In his book *The Power of Habit*, Charles Duhigg says that learning a "keystone habit" can help change other habits.

> Q: What in the world is a keystone habit?

> A: Some examples are stopping smoking, starting yoga, training for a marathon, participating in charities, or learning a new skill or art. One of the most powerful of all keystone habits, which we refer to as a Super Habit, is meditation.

Besides Smith himself, and sometimes his family, the main characters in our Smith Saga books are Linc St. Claire, Dame Georgina St. George, and Chris, all of whom practice and recommend TM or Transcendental Meditation. See Resource Materials Section 2 and the Commentary on Chapter 7 for information about TM and other forms of meditation.

CHAPTER 4

The Hornets' Nest

Quite a bit later that afternoon, Smith is walking in the deep woods with Chris when they hear gunshots.

"It isn't hunting season," Chris says. "Somebody must be target shooting."

Smith looks at him. "By any chance, does Seraphim own a gun?"

"Oh, several. She's an accomplished markswoman. She even won a couple of national championships."

Smith's only response is a thoughtful, "Hmm."

At that moment a high caliber rifle cracks nearby. A heavy pine branch crashes to their feet, narrowly missing them. Picking it up, Chris examines the sharply jagged broken end.

"A bullet did this," he says soberly.

"Let's walk a little faster," suggests Smith.

"Excellent idea."

Another shot causes Smith's heart to pound like a bass drum. A huge hornets' nest plops on the ground beside them, its occupants erupting in a cloud of fury.

Both men yell, "RUN!"

Zigging and zagging in a futile attempt to avoid being stung, Chris leads Smith to a swampy pool where they plunge into rotting leaves and frog spawn to evade their insect tormentors.

They stay under the surface of the shallow pool as long as they can, peeking out of the dark brown water only to grab a quick breath and again submerge. But the hornets prove persistent, and in spite of being thickly coated in odoriferous green scum, they are stung repeatedly.

As if responding to some secret signal from nature, the hornets leave just as the sun sets, and the men stumble out of the muck. Exhausted, covered in decaying flora and quite possibly fauna, and virtually on fire, they make their way back to the cabin, where Chris helps Smith apply a poultice of healing herbs and mud.

They sink into a pair of ancient rocking chairs. Smith closes his one unstung eye, holding a cold damp washcloth up to his other burning orb.

Chris rocks slowly. After a while he asks, "Do you feel up to talking?"

"I welcome the distraction," Smith replies.

"All right. So, we spoke about the tools of Total Brain Coaching, and the first two letters of the word DHARMIC. The third letter, A, in DHARMIC stands for Action."

Smith laughs, "Seraphim sure got us into action!"

"She certainly did. And the quality of our action depends upon the quality of our attention."

He continues, "Attention is defined as the flow of our

consciousness, the flow of awareness. The problem is that many folks habitually put their attention on the negative side of life. They see the cup as half empty and they tend to experience themselves as victims of circumstance. Other people are able to focus on the positive. For them, the cup is always half full, and they have a more empowered perception of reality. The way you view the world becomes a habit that influences all of your behavior."

Smith nods. "I get it."

"Of course you do. You are a P Energy State person, and you're not afraid of taking responsibility for your actions. With," Chris pauses, "one notable exception."

Smith's uninjured eye regards him suspiciously. "What's that?"

"Your relationship with Seraphim."

Smith looks pained. "Do you have to remind me?"

"Regardless of your individual Energy State," Chris tells him, "there are certain kinds of situations and relationships that will test anyone. Even strong Ps are vulnerable to the deep emotional pain associated with the phenomenon of learned helplessness. It's a childhood stress we carry into adulthood. P Energy State people are capable of building strong psychological defenses and they don't behave like victims, but unresolved early issues can still plague them. Part of becoming a mature adult is being able to recognize these hidden negative forces, and learning to embrace your power, taking responsibility for your thoughts as well as your actions. How you react to a perceived attack, whether it's real or not, perpetuates your personal karma."

Smith responds strongly, "Well, what the Frakk am I

supposed to do?"

"Each situation is different, but the principle is the same: Never act in anger. To do that is a sign of weakness rather than strength, and always leads to further problems. What you want to do is change your brain state the quickest and simplest way possible. But first you have to understand who you are and what it is that will help you regain balance."

"That sounds like a lotta work," Smith mutters unhappily.

"Learning what triggers set you off and changing your habit response can be challenging," admits Chris. "And we'll go into the specifics later."

"Is it as much work for the other Energy States?"

"Each Energy State has its own vulnerability, which is shaped by early experiences. For a V Energy State person, as we mentioned, emotions are primary and it's almost impossible for them to compartmentalize. Since Vs are more sensitive, it requires more focused attention and greater energy for them to change a habit."

"How about K Energy State people?"

"They also have a hard time changing a habit, but not because their attention isn't focused. They tend to be stable emotionally, at least when they are in balance, and they're quite good at focusing. The problem is that they can become too fixed in their ways and they really really don't like change. They can do it, but you have to give them extra time.

"Each Energy State has its pluses and minuses, and each requires its own tools in order to successfully change habits."

"What can I do?" Smith asks.

Chris holds up his index finger, tapping the air to indicate that Smith should wait. "Here's a question for you. It may seem a little extreme, but, if you knew that you had only five years to live, what would be the number one change you would want to make?"

"I don't even have to think about it," Smith tells him. "The most important thing for me would be to spend more time with my family. Of course, I'd want to make sure they were well taken care of, and also that they were on a positive life path."

"Would that involve your making any changes in your life?"

Smith considers for a moment. "I have to say that I would definitely spend less time on the golf course and more time with the family."

"That's good. And what would your list include if you were told that you had another 20 years to live?"

"Then I'd probably want to improve my golf drive," says Smith. "It veers a little to the right and I've always wanted to hit a draw instead of a fade."

Chris grins. "Okay. The point is that where you put your attention depends on a number of factors. It depends on who you are, and what your Energy State is. It also depends on where you are in your life, what you have already accomplished and what you still want to accomplish. The goals of a younger person would be different. They may want to pursue a successful career and find their life partner."

"Yeah, those were my goals when I was young. I didn't

consider golf. My life was about achieving success and building a family."

"Evaluating and prioritizing your goals is a very useful process, no matter what Energy State you may be. It helps focus your attention on what is most important to you."

"I have to tell you," Smith says soberly, "being around Seraphim is incredibly stressful for me. She manages to push all my buttons. I don't know how I'll ever improve that relationship."

"I do understand," Chris tells him. "The deeper the stress, the more uncomfortable or painful it can be when that stress is triggered. Our brains are wired in a certain way in early childhood, and this becomes reinforced by our experience. If we were brought up in an unhappy or emotionally turbulent environment, we will probably have problems with relationships later on.

"The reaction of a P Energy State person to emotional triggers is often combative or controlling. A V Energy State person would likely respond by immediately becoming emotionally upset. And a K Energy State person could become stubborn, withdrawn, even depressed. Relationships depend on various factors and one of the most important is the way that different Energy States interact together."

"Thank goodness Margaret and I get along so well. She always has a calming effect on me, and I'm usually happy to say 'yes' to her because I trust her completely. With Seraphim, right away I want to fight back."

"I agree, John. Your wife's Tri-Energy State is an excellent balance for your P Energy State. The problem is that you and

Seraphim are both P Energy State people, and you are both frequently imbalanced. When the two of you get together, you're like cage fighters on steroids."

"Ha, I only wish I were a mixed martial arts fighter! But I'm not, and since Seraphim is an expert markswoman, what the Frakk can I do?"

"Change how you react to her. It won't be easy, because you have established a habitual way of reacting to her. Seraphim's behavior acts as a powerful trigger that causes you to become instantly imbalanced.

"So, you have to create a new habit and it helps to start small. BJ Fogg emphasizes this in his popular book, *Tiny Habits*.

"I will help you make a Habit Plan. And you can begin with a simple change, such as dramatically dialing down your overreaction to her."

"How in the world do I do that?"

"There are several ways. Start by taking a deep breath and counting to five—but do it very slowly. Say to yourself: One one-thousand, Two one-thousand, Three one-thousand, Four one-thousand, Five one-thousand. With each number, take a breath in and out. When you get to five, take a long relaxing breath."

"Okay, then what?"

"Then you are going to be completely non-responsive to Seraphim, no matter what horrible thing she might say to provoke you, and she will certainly provoke you. But it's not Seraphim, or anyone else who is important here. YOU are.

"Put your attention on yourself, and focus on your breath. Feel it moving slowly in and out of your body. As you continue to breathe, feel your heart area and allow yourself to quiet down inside. Remember, this is about you, not her. If your attention wanders, gently bring it back to your breath, your heart. Do not react or speak until you feel that you have regained some balance."

"Oh man, that would be so hard," says Smith despairingly.

"But," Chris looks at him inquiringly, "you want to change."

"I do! I'm just not sure I have the will power or the ability. I wish I could reach into my brain and change my Frakking circuits."

"If only it were that easy. These old circuits are so complex and deep in the brain's structure that even an 'open ego' surgeon couldn't fix them. It's going to require patience on your part."

"Not exactly my strong point."

"Not at the moment," Chris agrees. "The first thing you have to do is change your behavior in order to construct a new neural circuit that will support your positive habit."

"How do I do that?"

"Since every experience you have changes your brain, give yourself a new experience. When you meet with Seraphim's belligerence—do not react! It won't be easy, but the more often you can do it the easier it will get.

"There is also one supreme way to take advantage of how even a single experience of a Super Habit can result in positive changes in your brain."

Smith is puzzled. "What are you talking about?"

"The experience of meditation, specifically Transcendental Meditation or TM. Studies show a remarkable range of improvements—from success in business to ending long-term addiction. The adoption of this one Super Habit establishes a powerful new neural circuit that facilitates a cascade of positive changes."

"As usual," Smith sighs, "Margaret is right. The first thing I'm going to do when I get home, is start TM. You really think it will help my relationship with Seraphim?"

"I am sure it will do a lot more than that. But ingrained habits are not easy to change, so you will definitely have to put extra attention on your behavior with Seraphim."

"You're saying that TM will help me, but I still have to work on my hot buttons. I can do that! Dame Georgina showed me how to change my company and that worked."

"Exactly," Chris confirms. "And this takes us to the next letter, R, in DHARMIC, which has to do with your inner Rhythm. Relationship habits are the hardest to change and there may be times when you have to Reorganize and Reboot, especially with Seraphim. One thing I want you to do is create a simple daily questionnaire that lets you rate your reaction to Seraphim each day."

Smith's voice reveals both uneasiness and interest as he asks, "Like how many times I blow up at her?"

"Even if you blow up," Chris says, "the most important thing to ask yourself is, 'Did I do my best to keep my mouth shut and bear her onslaught in silence?' If you fail, see if you can learn from that experience. Is there anything more you could do? Maybe you will have to create a new habit that works better. This is all part of Reorganize and Reboot."

And he goes on, "Because you're a P Energy State person, you'll enjoy evaluating yourself and learning from your mistakes. For other types, it's not so easy and they might need a coach who understands their problems and who will empathize and encourage them.

"The M in DHARMIC is the fifth letter and in TBC Life Coaching it stands for maintaining your balance. You can do this either by Self Coaching, Personal Coaching, Group coaching, or Environmental coaching."

"I remember self coaching, personal coaching, and group coaching. Can you remind me what Environmental Coaching is?"

"Environmental Coaching," Chris tells him, "is being aware of the triggers in your environment. They can have a huge effect on your ability to change your habit. This brings us to the I in DHARMIC and the sixth step in TBC coaching, Improve and Integrate, which for you means identifying and dealing with your triggers.

"Knowing what triggers cause you to go out of balance can help you adopt a new habit. If you are trying to lose weight, for example, it's a good idea not to have junk food in the house. And think how difficult it must be for a smoker to stop smoking if his or her partner is smoking. Making the right changes in your environment makes it easier for you to adopt a new habit. The more self-motivated you are, the easier it is for you to make changes, but a well-trained coach can help all Energy States."

"Sometimes, I'm confused about what's actually motivating me."

"There are different kinds of motivation," Chris says, "and motivation which is based on inspiration and appreciation is more lasting than motivation based on fear and criticism."

"Yeah, I completely agree."

"The final C in DHARMIC in TBC Life Coaching," Chris explains, "stands for Celebrate. And when you consider all these steps together you celebrate and create coherence which we will consider later."

"All this thinking," Smith says, "is making me hungry. How about we go out and get a bite to eat?"

"I'd say yes, to having a bite to eat," Chris agrees. "No to going out. It's not safe for us to go anywhere right now."

"Unh," moans Smith. "How true."

I know Seraphim is gunning for us, he thinks. *But Dang, 'the best defense is a good offense' is my motto! Just one last payback—then I'll change.*

TROUBLE IN PARADISE

CHAPTER 4 COMMENTARY

Which Wolf Wins

Smith has agreed to work with Chris to adopt a simple habit. If Seraphim speaks harshly to him, the first thing he will do is to count to five, taking a deep breath, and say slowly: One one-thousand, Two one-thousand, Three one-thousand, Four one-thousand, Five one-thousand. This is his simple Habit Plan.

Improving our relationships is one of the most complex and difficult of all habits to change, and Chris wants Smith to begin the process with something which is relatively doable.

In this chapter, Smith continues to learn more about what is involved in making a positive habit change and discovers the other tools for habit change that are expressed in our acronym DHARMIC.

Let's look at each of the tools associated with the letters A, R, M, I, and C.

A

The letter A in DHARMIC, as it is used in TBC Life Coaching, stands for: Attention. Action depends upon attention. The more attention you put on something, the stronger it naturally becomes in your life. Many traditions illustrate this axiom with a story about two wolves who are in deadly conflict. One wolf is cruel, negative, and destructive, while the other is brave, compassionate, and altruistic.

> Q: Which wolf wins?
>
> A: The wolf you feed and nourish, in other words, what you put your attention on, grows stronger!

Let's go over the different kinds of attention displayed by each of the Energy States.

The attention of a V person can be precise but tends to move rapidly from one topic to another. V Energy State people are more sensitive than other types and may be overwhelmed by sensory information, such as too many choices. Pushing a V individual to learn a new habit can result in a strong emotional reaction. And if they become overly excited and out of balance, it will be very difficult for them to focus their attention on habit change.

How does the attention of a P person affect how they learn a new habit? The P person is primarily interested in goals and solutions. They can often make excellent leaders who love competition and are also focused on making improvement in their own lives. Time is important to a P person and they like having a set timeline when making changes. As we have pointed out, adopting a new habit is relatively easy for P Energy State people.

K Energy people tend to have a settled mind. But they tend to be very attached to regular routines and they don't react well to change. You can't rush them. They require more time to make decisions than the other Energy States, and will be better able to execute their Habit Plan if they have some help. This is especially true when they are imbalanced and become stubborn and resistant.

Chris describes how different Energy States interact with each other and explains why two P Energy State people, like Smith and Seraphim, are likely to compete and fight, especially when they are imbalanced. See Resource Materials Section 9 for a more detailed description of some of the different possible positive and negative interactions between Energy States. Section 10 of the Resource Materials focuses on how these relationships affect parenting and family life.

There are certain general recommendations which apply to all Energy States:

- Start your action with baby steps
- Change one habit at a time
- Don't divide your attention

- Adopt a keystone or Super Habit to make it easier for you to stay in balance and change habits

Tiny Habits and *Atomic Habits* are two habit change books which reinforce the point that it's better to start with easier habits. Ayurveda also emphasizes the value of taking small steps. A P Energy State person (like Mr. Smith) will naturally be overly ambitious and want to make big changes right away, but he will be much more successful if he begins with smaller, more attainable goals.

Another recommendation is to add a new habit to one that already exists. This is called "habit stacking."

A K individual might already have established a habit of taking walks twice a day. And if this person wants to add a simple habit of drinking more water to his or her daily routine, it will be easier to adopt the new habit, by habit stacking and drinking a glass of water after each walk.

Your environment makes a gigantic difference in your ability to successfully adopt a new habit. Habit change is a lot easier in a supportive and relaxed environment.

From an Ayurvedic perspective, it is easier and more natural for you to create a new habit if it is complementary to your particular Energy State. For example, young P Energy State individuals thrive on physical activity and enjoy challenges. They will be much more enthusiastic about adopting a new exercise program if it is associated with a goal like running a marathon, or doing 50 push-ups a day.

R

The letter R in DHARMIC, as it is used in TBC Life Coaching, stands for: Rhythm. Everyone knows that it is hard to start and maintain a new habit. It may take some reorganizing and rebooting of your life. Each year many new resolutions are made and yet few are retained. We need to be flexible and be ready to start again, maybe even with a new Habit Plan.

Each Energy Type has their own ability to stick to a new habit. V Energy Types enjoy variation, so it is hard for them to stick to a particular habit or routine.

V people need a lot of help in order to remain grounded and focused. If they go off their habit change plan (and they will), it will benefit them to have a partner, friend, or coach who can help calm and encourage them, and help them to create routines which nourish, please, and support them.

P Energy State people are very different from V and K. The have a strong sense of purpose and are goal-oriented. P people have no trouble following a new habit or routine as long they believe that it will help to accomplish their goals. They tend to view habit change as a personal competition, and therefore enjoyable. If they believe that a new habit change does not benefit their objectives and ambitions, they will soon abandon it.

With a slower, steadier inner rhythm than either V or P individuals, a K Energy State person feels protected and comforted by a fixed routine. Change can be very difficult and it is their nature to resist it. They need time and encouragement to adjust.

M

The next letter, M, in DHARMIC, as it is used in TBC Life Coaching, stands for: Maintaining Balance. Both modern and traditional medicine are now in agreement about the advantages of creating a balanced life with good daily and seasonal routines, which incorporates exercise, diet, and sleep habits. It is also agreed that stress management, especially meditation, is a vital addition to everyone's state of balance.

Having a good routine allows you to synchronize with the biorhythms of nature. Ayurveda and other traditional systems of medicine have long understood the significance of biorhythms and their importance to health, and this understanding is now recognized by modern medicine.

Your gut bacteria have their own biological rhythms. When researchers transferred the gut bacteria from jet-lagged mice into non jet-lagged (and germ-free) mice, the recipient mice developed both glucose intolerance and obesity. Recent research on the gut bacteria reveals not only the presence of daily rhythms, but also seasonal biorhythms. Again, it is interesting that Ayurveda fully addresses the importance of seasonal rhythms.

See Resource Materials Section 2 for more information on meditation and how it improves mental and physical health.

Simple changes in your daily routine can give you more energy and adaptability for habit change. See the Resource Materials Section 6 about lifestyle tips on sleep, exercise, and diet for each Energy State.

We suggest four types of coaching to help you create energy and balance in your life:

- Self Coaching
- Personal Coaching
- Group Coaching
- Environmental Coaching

These approaches provide feedback which reinforces new habits. It is important to note that when we mention Group Coaching, we don't mean mentoring or therapy. Total Brain Coaching does not attempt to advise clients on their skills or profession, or to resolve deep-seated psychological problems. These are jobs for professionals with specific training in these issues.

Self Coaching is something that everyone does, whether we are aware of it or not. But there are tools which can help the process. Keeping a journal or using an app may be helpful, and one simple and amazing tool that can help you monitor the balance of your Energy State is the procedure of Self Pulse assessment as taught in Maharishi AyurVeda. See Resource Materials Section 4.

Personal Coaching may be done by a partner or a friend, but it is generally better to use a professional coach. The process of change can be delicate, especially in the beginning, and a trained expert knows when and how to help. A personal coach helps you identify goals and milestones using active listening, and by asking powerful open-ended questions that stimulate insight and understanding. Changing a habit requires time, energy, and sometimes outside help.

Group Coaching can be in person or online. In both situations, being part of a group is useful because you can see how others are coping with the challenges of habit change.

Environmental Coaching can help you deal with some of the triggers that affect your ability to make positive change. Many habit experts emphasize that changing your environment is key to changing your habits. It will help if everyone in your immediate environment respects your desire to adopt a new positive habit.

I

The letter I in DHARMIC, as it is used in TBC Life Coaching, stands for: Improvement and Integration. We specifically focus here on Identifying and Dealing with Your Triggers, which is part of Environmental Coaching. It is almost inevitable to be upset by triggers, especially emotional triggers, when you are trying to improve a relationship. Constant feedback from a friend or coach gives you a different point of view. Bringing your attention to any improvement you are making helps support your new habit.

Marshall Goldsmith, in his book *Triggers,* emphasizes asking yourself active questions in order to evaluate your progress. Let's say that you are keeping a journal of your progress, and you ask yourself, "How am I doing with my new habit today?" This is an indirect question which allows you to make excuses. An active and more helpful approach might be, "Did I do my best to maintain my new habit today?" This question places the responsibility on you and emphasizes your honest effort.

Measurable outcomes are a critical part of any habit change plan. It's hard to determine success if it can't be measured. If you are trying to lose weight you have to step on the scale. Measuring outcomes also helps you keep track of what is working and what is not, allowing you to update your habit plan for improvement.

C

The letter C in DHARMIC, as it is used in TBC Life Coaching, stands for: Celebrate. This is the same as in *Total Brain Coaching*. There are many things we can do to celebrate. Every time you make a change, for example, even if it's only a mini success, reward yourself with a suitable celebration. For bigger milestones, celebrate once a week, once a month, or once a year.

Researchers at Harvard have examined what motivates employees to produce the greatest creative output. What they found was that the old motivators of fear and pressure were not associated with higher performance, but happiness and inner positive emotions were. When it comes to habit change, motivation really is everything.

What happens to your brain when you become motivated? We already know that anticipating a reward is a powerful motivator. In the brain, this is reflected in what is called the dopamine feedback loop. Dopamine is a neurotransmitter involved in all types of behavior, including motivation. Dopamine used to be thought of as the pleasure chemical of the brain. We have learned, however, that dopamine is actually the basis of the anticipation of, or craving for, pleasure. Dopamine causes you to seek experiences which you think will make you happy.

Every time you post a selfie, eat chocolate, smoke a cigarette, or play a video game, you are turning on your ravenous dopamine feedback loop. This is the brain mechanism that goes into action whenever you encounter a trigger that causes you to anticipate gratification. It allows you to experience a surge of dopamine, but it is never enough. Psychologists suggest that dopamine is the basis of all addiction, from drugs to social media. And science has found that the areas in the brain dedicated to anticipation are larger than those which have to do with actual pleasure.

When we are addicted to something unhealthy, this feedback loop leads to a negative result. But instead of putting your attention on eliminating old negative habits, it is far easier to replace them with new positive habits. Your dopamine feedback loop has the power to provide you with the motivation which allows you to establish and maintain new positive habits.

Learning to meditate, for example, creates coherence in the brain and a new experience of happiness and peace. There are many other habits we can learn which create health and happiness in our lives.

Changing one habit is the beginning, but small wins lead to big wins. Once you improve one part of your life, you will inevitably want to adopt some other positive habit. And the act of celebration helps to reinforce your positive feedback loop, which in turn increases your motivation and self-confidence.

If you read the book *Total Brain Coaching,* you will have noticed that the seven principles given are slightly different from the 7 Steps of TBC Life Coaching. For an explanation of how these two systems relate to each other, see Final Commentary: Applying Total Brain Coaching to Your Life.

CHAPTER 5

The Bath From Hell

It's almost eleven the next morning by the time Smith appears at Chris's cabin. As he walks in, the older man regards him appraisingly.

"So, John, what have you been up to this morning?"

Smith's eyes open wide: *I saw the guy levitate. Is he also telepathic?*

Without waiting for an answer, Chris suggests invitingly, "Ready for a canoe ride?"

Relieved to be on a safe subject, Smith replies, "Sure am."

Once they're out on the lake, he can't contain himself and launches into an account of his morning escapade. "I snuck into Seraphim's cottage while she was shopping with Margaret."

For a couple of seconds, Chris says nothing, then he asks, "What did you hope to achieve?"

"I just wanted to leave her a little gift."

"You left a present?"

"Yeah, a gift that goes on giving," chortles Smith. "I went into her bathroom and poured a small essential oil offering into her bottle of bubble bath."

"That was nice of you."

"No," Smith corrects him. "It was sneaky, mean, maybe even cruel." He feels simultaneously ashamed and proud of himself.

"I don't understand."

"When I was young," Smith turns around on his seat to tell him, "I once made the mistake of adding half a bottle of wintergreen oil to my bath. And to this day, the experience is burned into my consciousness. The thing is, when you first get into the tub after adding the wintergreen, you lay back and enjoy the pleasant clean smell. But in a minute, it's like you're bathing in fire and you can't get out fast enough. Even when you are all dried off, your skin continues to scream."

Ignoring the expression on Chris's face, he continues, "I thought that it was a suitable payback for what Seraphim did to us with the hornets' nest, *quid pro quo*. I know that I went against your advice, but I had to do it."

Chris doesn't say anything for some moments and Smith stares at him uncomfortably.

Finally, Chris says, "I understand, but you do realize that you might have created an even bigger hornets' nest? And, of course, this escalates the conflict between you."

"Oh sure, I know that," Smith says blithely. He laughs, "Bring it on."

Chris frowns slightly. "You seem pleased with yourself."

Smith says nothing, and Chris continues, "I'm honestly not sure if you're ready for the next part of the TBC Life Coaching program."

"Hey, now that I've settled the score with Seraphim, you bet I'm ready. As I said, she's shopping with Margaret for the day, so we don't have worry about immediate retaliation." He is obviously very pleased with himself.

"And," he adds, "it's unlikely that she will take a bath until later this evening or tomorrow morning."

"So," Chris says, "you've bought yourself one more day before…what?" He pauses. "Hell descends?"

Smith looks at him sheepishly. "I didn't think that far in advance."

"And that could be a problem," Chris tells him. "But there's no point in lecturing you on the consequences of your actions because tomorrow you are going to be living them." He paddles smoothly. "There's nothing like real experience to get across a theoretical point."

"Hey, tomorrow I'll come up with a great new plan," Smith says buoyantly. "What shall we talk about today?" he asks, paddling happily.

"Maintaining balance," Chris tells him, giving weight to each word.

"Maintaining your mental and physical balance is the key to success in everything. Do you remember what it takes for a P Energy State person to stay in balance?"

"Yeah, yeah, yeah, of course I do. You, Dame Georgina, and Linc St. Claire, have hammered away about it."

He recites, "The two main triggers that cause a P Energy State person to become imbalanced are not eating on time and getting overheated."

Chris studies the back of Smith's head. "Did you happen to skip breakfast this morning?"

"Y'know," Smith says thoughtfully, "I did miss breakfast. But I feel fine, and I believe that what I did to Seraphim was completely justified. I think it was exactly the right thing under the circumstances."

"Ahh, self-righteousness—one of the common characteristics of an out of balance P Energy State, which I may not have mentioned yet."

Smith protests, "I'm never self-righteous."

"Oh, I see," says Chris flatly.

Smith crows, "This is full-out war, and I'm havin' a ball."

"I'm sure you are," Chris comments. "Why don't we talk about something else? Do you have any idea what makes a V Energy State person become imbalanced?"

"Nah, I don't remember much about V Energy States." He laughs, "They're not my type."

"V Energy State people, like your dear niece," Chris reminds him, "are very sensitive and easily become overstimulated."

"Oh, yeah," Smith responds agreeably, "I always felt bad that Chloe has to cope with Seraphim on a daily basis."

"Over the years," Chris explains, "Chloe has had to develop certain protective tactics in order to deal with her mother's imbalanced P Energy State. The problem is that she loves you both, and your battle with Seraphim only makes her life more difficult."

"I never thought about that." Smith scratches the top of his

THE BATH FROM HELL

head. "You're right. I don't want that sweet girl to suffer collateral damage. It's not like she's a K or P Energy State person."

"Actually," Chris tells him, "a K Energy State person requires extra stimulation to stay balanced."

"Maybe a little of Seraphim's wintergreen bubble bath oil would get them going. It's highly invigorating." He roars with laughter.

Chris lays his paddle on the floor of the canoe. As if he's experiencing a bad headache, he pinches the bridge of his nose. "Are you finished?"

"I suppose," says Smith reluctantly. "I'm just having too dang much fun today."

"Enjoy it while you can," Chris murmurs under his breath. "And remember," he cautions, "whatever you put your attention on becomes more powerful. If you put your attention on revenge and hostility, that's what will dominate your life."

"I suppose," Smith says grudgingly.

"If you want this war between you and Seraphim to end, you have to adopt a new mindset, a new style of dealing with her. Isn't that what you want?"

"Well, yeah, I thought I did."

Chris goes on, "Once you start to change how you react to her, everything else will begin to fall into place."

"Ah, I dunno, it sounds impossible."

"It's all about where you put your attention. Did Linc tell you about his friend who coached the Swedish women's golf team?"

"Now there's a topic," Smith holds his paddle with one hand, jabbing the air emphatically with his other index finger, "I'm really interested in."

"Linc's friend is Kjell Enhager, a motivational speaker and international sports coach who often appears on Nick Faldo's golf show."

"Cool," says Smith.

"Before Kjell helped coach the Swedish team, they were ranked 20th in the world. By the time he finished, they were ranked Number 1."

"What the Frakk did he do?"

"He changed the mindset of the entire team. Kjell and the other coaches used various strategies, but this was the most important."

"But how did he do it?"

"You know how easy it is to focus on mistakes while you are playing."

"I am only too familiar with the phenomenon. After each round I think about my bad shots and analyze the heck out of them, trying to figure out what I did wrong."

"That's very common. But Kjell had the players put their attention only on their best shots after each round. And the results were dramatic."

"Oh, yeah. Now I remember Dame Georgina telling me about them. She encouraged me to do something similar in order to change the mindset of my company. And I gotta say, it worked phenomenally."

"It's a similar situation in your personal life—you want to

redirect the focus of your attention from retaliation and one-upmanship, to improving your relationships."

"But I have no idea how to begin."

"You start by restoring your own balance. I'm thinking that it might help if you could play some golf."

"Oh," Smith gasps delightedly, "that would be a life saver. But where can I play?"

"I think I know a place where you can at least practice."

"Where?"

"A friend of mine," Chris tells him, "has a very nice open field. I'll call him today and see if he will cut the grass for us. It's a far cry from the manicured greens of a country club but you'll be able to hit some balls."

Smith is excited. "I can practice my short game. Call him, please!"

"All right, but you have to be very discreet because my friend leases the land from Seraphim."

Smith folds his mouth inward. "My lips are sealed."

"So," Chris continues, "shall we talk a little more about being in balance?"

"Carry on!" commands Smith.

"A good daily routine," Chris tells him, "makes a big difference in life. For example, did you get enough sleep last night?"

"Well, no. I was up late thinking about my strategy, but I really don't feel that fatigue hurts my decision-making ability."

Chris utters a short silent laugh. "You're missing the big picture, John.

"First of all, what did I say about fatigue being the enemy? You never want to make an important decision when you are tired. An exhausted brain does not operate efficiently. You don't race your car and expect to win on half a tank of gas."

"Maybe not, but my revenge plan is a dinger!"

"I have a question for you," says Chris. "Is revenge going to improve your relationship?"

"Well, what the Frakk else can I do?"

"Learn to how to interact positively with Seraphim."

"How?"

"By learning to stay in balance, and there are several things you can do to make that happen. I know that Margaret is helping your diet. And while you're up at the lake, swimming in the cold water will help balance your P Energy and also give you a little exercise. For me, meditation is the magic wand. You might like to think of it as the big gun.

"However you do it—and I recommend that you make use of every available resource—keeping your Energy State balanced will improve your relationships enormously."

"Even with Seraphim?"

"Especially with Seraphim," Chris confirms.

"Everything has to do with how your brain is wired. As a P Energy State person, it's your nature to be competitive and aggressive at times, so you need to find ways to ensure that your brain circuits don't get overheated and overloaded.

"At this point, Seraphim brings out the worst in you. We're not going to go into why she does it. There could be a number of reasons. But she has become your 'bête noire,' your black dog, as Sir Winston Churchill used to refer to his dark moods. And if you learn how to behave more positively in your relationship with her, it's going to help you manage other challenging relationships."

"Oh, I get it," says Smith. "Seraphim is my 'worthy opponent,' the way Michael Jordon saw his greatest rivals in *The Last Dance*."

"That's a good analogy, but perhaps you don't have to perceive Seraphim as an opponent."

"Yeah?" Smith is skeptical.

"Look at your relationship with Seraphim as an opportunity to learn how to control your deeper emotions. But as I said, before you can change how you interact with her, you first have to rewire your brain."

"Wait, how do I do that?"

"You know now that experience changes your brain. It is literally rewiring itself each moment. And every time you adopt a new habit, it becomes rewired. Think of how tricky it is to ride a bicycle at first. But the more you do it, the easier it gets. Once new neural circuits are formed in specific parts of your brain, they begin to be automatic. Your neurophysiology is human anatomy in action.

"It's like your golf swing—once you know the fundamentals and practice enough, it becomes easier and easier. Of course, it's important for you to have a good teacher and to learn the correct fundamentals. You have had an ideal golf teacher in Linc St. Claire."

Smith beams.

"The routines of the finest athletes are so deeply established in their brain physiology that they can be supremely confident and able to spontaneously enter the 'zone.' "

"Oh yeah," says Smith. "Dame Georgina told me about samurai warriors and baseball stars who could effortlessly enter the zone in moments of intense competition."

"Athletes talk about going into the zone," Chris continues. "But when your neural circuits for emotions are rewired and firing coherently, you will be able to begin to have a similar zone experience."

The sun is in the west as they edge the canoe beside the dock. Smith is starting to feel good about committing to improving his relationship with his sister-in-law, but this positive possibility shatters as he realizes that she's probably back from shopping and stepping into the bubble bath from hell.

CHAPTER 5 COMMENTARY

Maintaining Balance

In this chapter Smith once again emphasizes the fourth step: Maintaining Balance. Being in balance produces energy, and quite a lot of energy is required to make successful habit change. Why? Because habit change involves rewiring your brain.

Staying in balance and having good energy is the foundation of all positive behavior in your life: health, emotional stability, personal relationships, job performance, creativity, and self-motivation.

Paying attention to your Energy State is about being self-aware, and knowing which triggers cause you to go out of balance and how to deal with them. If you are constantly busy, constantly involved in activity, it's hard, if not impossible, to be aware of, or to effect, changes in your Energy State. Certain techniques help you become more self-aware—meditating, keeping a journal, and Self Pulse. See Resource Materials Section 4 for a detailed description on how to do Self Pulse assessment.

Staying in Balance

How can you stay in balance? To answer this, let's look at a few areas of our daily life from the perspective of the three main Energy States—V, P, and K.

Sleep

Enough sleep is necessary to clear away toxins that build up in your brain during the day. Numerous studies correlate the lack of sleep with poor mental performance and health problems. How much sleep you need depends on several factors, and the most basic is your personal Energy State.

V Energy State people frequently have a hard time going to sleep and are very susceptible to insomnia. They need to understand that they must avoid excessive stimulation before bedtime and take real steps to wind down and relax, such as having a warm bath, listening to peaceful music, and using calming aromatherapy.

A P Energy State person tends to go to sleep quickly. But when the P person goes out of balance, he or she can experience difficulty sleeping.

K Energy State individuals almost never have trouble falling asleep, but they often have a hard time getting up in the morning.

Diet and Digestion

We have discussed the importance of the gut-brain axis and its impact on energy and mental health. Improving your digestion and eating the most suitable food for your Energy State will be a great help to keep you in good balance.

The appetite of a V person tends to be irregular and their digestive power is strong at one time and weak at another. Everyone likes to snack, but a V benefits from eating several small but nutritious meals throughout the day, rather than three "solids." It is especially important for a V to eat in a quiet environment, away from distractions and stress. When their gut is balanced, the V digestion is quite good. When the V gut is out of balance, the individual may experience symptoms such as indigestion, gas, and constipation.

The defining characteristic of the P Energy State is a strong digestive fire. The digestive power of all Energy States is strongest at noon, and it is best for all of them to eat their largest and heaviest meal at this time. But the P gut is programmed to produce an especially powerful appetite, so it's necessary for them to eat a good amount, on time, every day, or they will experience physical discomfort, and quite possibly, emotional turmoil or anger. When the P gut is balanced, digestion is highly efficient; but when it is out of balance, the person can experience hyperacidity and indigestion.

K Energy State individuals have a good steady digestion, and it doesn't bother them to miss an occasional meal. The K Energy State person loves food, but because they have a slower metabolism, they will gain weight easily, and must be careful to eat only moderate amounts.

See *The Rest And Repair Diet: Heal Your Gut, Improve Your Physical and Mental Health, and Lose Weight* for details about specific dietary recommendations for your Energy State.

Exercise

Modern medicine recognizes the value of regular exercise and scientific studies validate its benefits. Nevertheless, in spite of our good intentions, most of us spend too much time sitting and not enough time moving and stretching.

V individuals enjoy exercise that involves moving quickly and/or gracefully, but their physiology is not suited for endurance sports. They are sprinters rather than marathoners and must be very careful not to get overtired. Activities like dancing, paddleboarding, yoga—anything that keeps them moving easily—is excellent for a V. They do well with a gentle-to-moderate, grounding, warming workout.

P Energy State individuals are usually highly competitive, and they don't hold back. Possessing stamina and strength, they are often drawn to organized sports. They are also goal-oriented and often overdo exercise, paying the consequences later. Above all, P people need to avoid becoming overheated. Active water sports like swimming, surfing, and canoeing are all good for them. If you see somebody out parasailing, that person will almost certainly prove to be a P Energy State type.

K individuals generally have good endurance and strength, and regular active physical exercise is necessary to keep them from becoming overweight and lethargic (i.e. couch potatoes). Running, jogging, and energetic gym workouts are all very beneficial.

Yoga is one of the easiest, most popular forms of exercise, and it benefits every Energy State. Research shows that yoga postures, or asanas, improve both physical and psychological health. Choose whichever form of yoga best suits your individual Energy State, age, and needs. We recommend the Maharishi Yoga Asana program because it is especially respectful of your body and supports the experience of transcendence.

Stress

Every human on earth can benefit from meditation and because of its many positive results, we recommend Transcendental Meditation. See Resource Materials Section 2.

Summary

V Energy State

V Energy State individuals are generally bright and they learn quickly. They are also good at creating new ideas and projects. When they become imbalanced, they easily become oversensitive and fatigued, and may also experience mood swings.

Although V people generally dislike routines, a good routine is critical for them to be able to maintain balance. See Resource Materials Section 1.

IMBALANCE IN THE V ENERGY STATE	
Causes of V Imbalance	
Overstimulation	Too many choices
Overexertion	Negative emotions
Irregular routine	Stressful situations
Cold and/or windy weather	Unpleasant interactions with others
Excessive travel	
Signs of V Imbalance	
Hyperactivity	Restless
Easily distracted	High strung
Overly emotional	Forgetful
Anxious	Poor digestion
Nervous	Constipation
Fearful	Irregular appetite
Lonely	Spacey
Quickly changing moods	
Recommendations To Balance V Energy State	
Establish and maintain a daily routine	Take extra rest to recharge
Avoid cold, windy weather	Have healthy and delicious snacks
Reduce excessive stimulations	Create a bedtime routine
Guard against fatigue	Enjoy creative activities
Focus on specific goals	

P Energy State

P Energy State people usually have a lot of energy and staying power. They tend to be highly organized, possessing a strong and penetrating intellect, and are often good decision-makers. They are drawn to positions of leadership. It's no coincidence that many top businesspeople and athletes are frequently P individuals. When a P is imbalanced, they have trouble controlling their anger, and at the very least, can be irritable and bossy. They may also be impatient, difficult to interact with, and controlling. The secret for a P person to stay in good balance is simply for them to eat the right foods on time, and not become overheated. See Resource Materials Section 1.

IMBALANCE IN THE P ENERGY STATE	
Causes of P Imbalance	
Overheating Not eating on time Not drinking enough water Negative emotions	Overly competitive or aggressive situations Hot spices such as chilies
Signs of P Imbalance	
Irritable Angry Impatient Critical Jealous Hostile Obsessive-compulsive behaviors	Intense hunger Excessive thirst Sensitivity to spicy and/or fried foods, with indigestion and/or heartburn Excessive sweating Temper tantrums

Recommendations To Balance P Energy State	
Eat on time, especially at lunch	Enjoy physical activity during the day
Prevent overheating	On hot days turn on air conditioning
Keep well-hydrated	
Avoid foods with "hot" spices	On mild days keep the windows open

K Energy State

K Energy State people are generally steady and tend to carefully consider any decision. They don't easily become upset and are often patient, easygoing, and agreeable. When they go out of balance, however, they can be stubborn, or lethargic and depressed. The main strategy for a K person to stay in good balance is to keep physically active and mentally stimulated.

IMBALANCE IN THE K ENERGY STATE	
Causes of K Imbalance	
Too little activity	Exposure to excessively hot, humid weather
Lack of mental stimulation	
Lack of regular exercise	Exposure to cold, damp weather
Overeating	Excessive sleep
Signs of K Imbalance	
Stubborn	Sad
Depressed	Withdrawn
Lethargic	Excess mucus
Lazy	Weight gain
Recommendations To Balance K Energy State	

Keep mentally and physically stimulated	Try not to overeat: light meals are best
Include regular outdoor activity and exercise	Allow extra time for everything

These simple tips for keeping each Energy State in good balance are very beneficial when they are incorporated into your daily routine.

TROUBLE IN PARADISE

CHAPTER 6

The Honey Trap

Smith finally falls asleep before dawn after a restless night. The sound of Margaret's voice wakes him several hours later.

"Oh, I'm so sorry," she is saying into her phone, "you poor thing. I have a bottle of rose hydrosol that Chloe can bring over to you. Spray it on your rash a few times a day to help cool and soothe it."

As Smith listens, he feels a conflicting rush of guilt and delight. He wonders if he's a bad person, and quickly justifies his behavior to himself...*What I did isn't that different from dropping a hornets' nest on somebody's head!*

Wearily swinging his legs around the edge of the bed, he sits up.

"Seraphim won't be joining us for lunch," Margaret tells him. "She has a terrible rash all over her body. I wonder if it's an allergic reaction."

"Uh-huh," he mumbles. "Too bad."

Pausing for long moment, he adds, "I'm thinking that I might have a bite and then amble over to Chris's, if that's all right with you?"

"Of course. I'm so glad you two are becoming friends."

After a hearty lunch, Smith walks around the lake to Chris's cabin. He finds him splitting wood outside.

Chris looks up. "How is everyone doing this fine day?"

"Well, Margaret's fine. I'm fine." He waits a beat. "Seraphim has a little rash."

Chris stares at him. "What do you think she'll make of it?"

Smith shrugs, "She's no dummy. I expect she'll add 2 plus 2 and get 4. And the second she recovers she'll retaliate with full force."

Chris shakes his head. "Action and reaction," he says quietly. "It's the law of karma."

Smith ignores this comment. "Any news from your farmer friend?" he asks. "I'm ready to distract myself with a little golf."

"He called this morning to say that he's just cut the grass." Chris pauses. "Do you really think it's wise for you to be out and about?"

"I'm pretty sure Seraphim won't be doing much today," Smith replies confidently.

"All right then. Do you have clubs with you?"

"Not a one. That was part of my agreement with Margaret, no dang clubs at the lake."

"I have a few Cleveland wedges you could use," Chris tells him. "I may even have an old bag of balls."

"Perfect!" crows Smith.

"I'll drop you off and pick you up later," Chris promises. "The farmer wants me to go over some legal papers with him as a return favor. It shouldn't take more than an hour or so."

They climb into an old Range Rover and bump down a rough dirt track for about fifteen minutes until an abandoned farm appears in the middle of thick woods. Behind three decrepit buildings, Smith sees a broad, recently mowed meadow.

"You should know," Chris informs him, "that there's no cell phone reception here."

"No problem," says Smith, taking out the golf gear.

Before Chris is out of sight, he begins to hit a series of balls into the middle of the clearing. The blue sky is filled with puffy white clouds. The sun is shining. Birds are singing. Smith is as happy as if he were playing on the finest golf course in the world. Striking his last ball with a satisfying smack, he walks to the center of the field to collect the balls, and wonders at the large number of fat black flies which have landed on them. Bending over, he picks one up to examine it. It's sticky, gooey even, with several flies stuck in it as if in amber.

Looking down at his feet, he sees that he is standing in the middle of a large viscous glob of what appears to be honey. Again he bends down, and sticks his thumb into the stuff experimentally. He licks it...*Yeah, honey.*

From the main golden mass of the sweet stuff, several trails spread out in different directions, like rays of golden sun leading into the forest. *What the...?*

He doesn't have long to think about it because right then two small black bear cubs waddle out of the trees. They are licking, sniffing, and voraciously consuming the honey, following its irresistible trail in his direction.

They're coming straight at me. And, uh-oh, where there are cubs there's always a Momma!

He drops the club and the ball, turns on his heel, and runs into the surrounding woods in the opposite direction. He's looking for a climbable tree, but as he pounds through the brush, he remembers that bears are good climbers, and veers into deeper woods. He is hoping to get far away from the cubs before mother makes her appearance.

Thinking he hears something behind him, he runs even faster, feet thudding into the earth, breaking branches, swooshing leaves, kicking stones. *The mother bear is after me!*

Swerving between evergreens, he climbs a hill. Almost at the top of the rise, he stops and bends over, gasping for breath. His side stabs him painfully and his heart is beating so hard it makes his eyeballs jiggle.

He can't hear anything behind him now and slowly makes it up the last few feet to where the ground is flat again and slumps down to catch his breath. Surveying the landscape below, all he can see are the tops of trees. The field is completely hidden, and grim reality strikes. *I'm frakking lost.*

After a few more hours of wandering, Smith notices that the sun is lower than it was, and it's moved west considerably. Frustrated and exhausted, he drops his weary body to the ground. *It's going to be dark soon, and the last thing I want is to be stranded in the woods at night.*

He has no idea what kind of animals might be around. *If*

there are bears, he reasons, *there could be wolves.*

He shudders and reflects on the circumstances that led him to this moment. *What's a bunch of honey doing in a field anyway? And why do all those paths of honey lead almost deliberately from the woods to the center of the field? Is the farmer trying to catch something?*

It's odd, he thinks, *very odd. Too dang odd!*

He remembers what Chris told him—the land was being leased from Seraphim, and that he would have to be circumspect in his request to the farmer.

That's it. The farmer is under Seraphim's thumb and must have reported Chris's request back to her. She knows perfectly well that golf is my weakness, in this case, my Frakking Achilles heel. She would know immediately why Chris wanted to use the field. I bet she manipulated the farmer to get Chris out of the way. Dang, she's good!

He has another thought: *That rash of hers must be very uncomfortable, how could she have set up the honey trap for me?*

He answers his own question. *Obviously, the farmer must have spread the honey. But doesn't she care that the mother bear might maul or even kill me? What the Frakk was she thinking?*

A word comes to him—*Revenge.*

He wants to laugh, but it's getting dark now and there is a chill in the air. . He racks his brain trying to recall what little he ever knew about survival in the woods. He's watched enough reality shows to know that the first thing to do is build a shelter. Busy gathering pine branches, he stops short when he hears howling in the distance.

Is it wolves?

The howls get closer. *They're on my Frakking trail!*

In the last remaining light, he searches for a pointed branch to use as a weapon. *I'm not going down without a fight.*

Finding a stout one, he crouches and prepares for action.

Seraphim might at least regret knowing she caused my death, he thinks. *And Margaret and the rest of the family will never forgive her.*

He is composing his obituary when a voice shouts over the baying, "John, where are you?"

It's Chris!

"Over here," he shouts as the howling grows louder. "Come quick, the wolves are almost on me."

With throaty growls and overeager yips three beasts emerge from the brush. Smith stares through the gloom. *They aren't wolves. They're Huskies!*

Chris steps past the animals. "Are you all right?"

"Yes, and am I glad to see you!" Smith exclaims as three large drooling dogs—*They really do look a lot like wolves!*—come right up to him, whining ingratiatingly and yipping softly, wanting to be patted. Twining themselves around him, they lean their powerful bodies against him, almost knocking him over.

Chris whistles to the dogs, who immediately sit at attention. Taking off his padded jacket, he puts it around Smith's shoulders. "We were worried about you."

"I was completely lost," Smith laughs.

"You're actually very close to the cabin. Paradise Lake is on the other side of the next rise, minutes away. You must have an inborn sense of direction.

"Let's get you warm and we'll call Margaret. She's very worried. Even Seraphim called asking about you."

When he finally got home, Smith gave his very relieved wife a detailed account of how he became lost, carefully leaving out any mention of Seraphim's part in the honey trap. Margaret understood how important it was not to get between a mother and her cubs and congratulated him on his survival skills.

The next morning, he tells Chris the whole story.

"I did warn you," Chris reminds him, "about escalating the confrontation."

"Yeah," Smith has to admit, "you did. Who would have thought that Seraphim would turn out to be some sort of strategic general, armed with the knowledge of guerrilla warfare? Now I've got to figure out how to get back at her."

"You haven't learned your lesson yet?" asks Chris incredulously.

"Whaddya mean?"

"This is a war you can't win. Seraphim takes no prisoners."

"Well, what am I supposed to do? Lie down in defeat?"

"No, the important thing is not to lose your head. You need to be clear minded and sharper than ever."

"Yeah, so I can come up with a swift retaliation."

"No," Chris says emphatically. "This is the time for you to check in with yourself."

"Meaning?"

"Feel your body right now. Is your Energy State in or out of balance?"

"I'd say out of balance and getting madder by the minute."

"An honest assessment," Chris comments. "If you know that you are out of balance, you also know that this is not the time to make a decision. It is time, however, to change your brain state. You want to regain your balance, so you can be calm and cool, mentally and physically. Being impulsive will only lead to further problems."

"Sure, but striking back as fast and hard as I can, will at least give me some Frakking gratification."

"Fanning a fire makes it grow stronger. Before you do anything, John, you have to cool your P Energy State and then regroup. A swim will help. When you submerge your overheated brain in cold water, your frontal cortex will come back online and override the unreasonable emotional circuits dominating your behavior. Your Energy State will change spontaneously from unbalanced to balanced.

"Give it a try," he urges. "A couple of hours won't affect your plans much one way or the other."

"All right," Smith agrees. "You rescued me last night, so I owe you something. I'll try and cool down, but don't expect miracles."

Over the next few hours they swim in the lake, eat a good meal together, and go for a long walk.

Smith's reasoning powers return. "I'm feeling a lot better," he tells Chris.

"Now that your brain has cooled down, I suggest that you use it to make a good choice."

"I'm ready," says Smith. "And I choose…to counterattack!"

Chris muffles a groan. "Before you make that choice, John, please consider the consequences. If you attack again, what do you think that Seraphim will do?"

"Without a doubt, she will attack me again." Smith is almost nonchalant.

"Do you think that this time it's possible that her response might have more serious consequences?"

"I dunno. I suppose, but I'll handle it."

"Consider her history," Chris tries to reason with him. "First, she launches a naval attack, then an artillery attack, and finally, animal warfare. She could go nuclear this time," he pauses, "and what about collateral damage?"

"You mean like Margaret?"

"Margaret and Chloe."

"Hmm, so, you're talking about repercussions."

"Exactly. Are you willing to sacrifice others in your desire for revenge?"

Smith considers this. "I guess not. I know Margaret wouldn't be happy with me, that's for sure."

"Okay, the stakes are high. Now, having considered the consequences of your proposed action, would you like to make a different choice?"

"Is this a part of your coaching thing, trying to get me to surrender and end the war?"

"I'm trying to coach you so that you can make a positive choice and end your destructive confrontation with Seraphim, or at least begin a period of detente. I'm not telling you anything that you don't already know."

"Let's say that, in theory, I agree with what are you proposing."

"It's your life, John. You are a very successful and well-rounded individual who came to me wanting to make positive changes."

Well-rounded, thinks Smith. *Is he referring to my character or my waist?*

Chris goes on, "What I'm suggesting is that you sleep on the possibility of a new approach to this old problem, then we can continue to strategize."

"I'm not sure that a night's sleep is going to change my desire for revenge. Out of respect for you, though, I'll suspend my plans until tomorrow."

Walking back to the cottage to be with Margaret, he thinks to himself, *Chris's advice is probably right. But revenge is so Frakking sweet!*

CHAPTER 6 COMMENTARY

Fight or Flight

Smith is in fight-or-flight mode for much of this chapter. One particular area in Smith's brain, the amygdala, immediately becomes activated as soon as he imagined an angry mother bear. Our greatest fears and phobias are stored in the amygdala. Once it is triggered, the amygdala prevents information from going to higher logic centers in our prefrontal cortex. Instead, it sends serious threat signals to the hypothalamus and the adrenal glands. Your heart beats faster, your blood pressure rises, blood flow increases in your muscles, adrenalin flows throughout your body, and your brain becomes hyperalert.

To some degree everyone experiences the effects of stress every day, but it is generally caused by something less threatening than a bear. Oddly enough, many of us have actually become addicted to stress, which is not good since the effects of prolonged stress are harmful. Maintaining higher resting levels of the stress hormone cortisol is associated with a suppression of the immune system and the destruction of cells in our hippocampus, an area of the brain that is responsible for both memory and emotional regulation. Excessive stress has a negative impact on everything in our lives, especially on our relationships.

Smith shows us a perfect example of this. At this point, his threat network has gone crazy and he is consumed with revenge. Fortunately, he has a very good coach who doesn't push any of Smith's P Energy triggers. Chris's main advice is: Maintain Balance. He makes use of simple tips from Ayurveda, suggesting that Smith cool physically and mentally down by taking a dip in the icy lake water, and he makes sure that Smith swims around and ducks his head under for a few seconds. Then he feeds him and ensures that he is rested before giving him further advice. And when he does give advice, it's in the form of questions which will allow Smith to reach positive conclusions on his own.

Only when Smith's brain is balanced does Chris encourage self-awareness by asking him how he thinks Seraphim feels. Smith's empathy level, however, is on empty. Chris points out that if he continues on his current path of destruction, collateral damage may ensue that could harm Margaret and Chloe. Smith agrees not to make any decisions until he's had another night's rest.

CHAPTER 7

Damage Control

Smith thinks about choices and consequences all night long, and when he gets to Chris's cabin in the morning, he is grateful for the rich strength of his host's coffee.

After eating a light breakfast together, they agree to go canoeing. This time, Chris seats Smith in the stern.

He wants me to steer? Smith wonders. He doesn't have a clue how to do it.

Unlooping the bow line from the metal cleat, Chris tells him to slip off the stern line, which he does.

Chris uses his paddle to gently push the canoe away from the dock. Turning to face Smith he holds it up.

"Think of your paddle as a rudder," he tells him. "The angle of the rudder is what determines the direction of the boat." He demonstrates, using his wrists to turn his paddle one way and then the other, altering the angle of its face.

Smith dips his own paddle in the water and experiments by twisting his bottom wrist, turning the paddle in a radius of almost 180 degrees.

"You don't have to turn the paddle quite so radically to get the canoe to respond," his mentor tells him. "And you don't have to twist the blade until your stroke is almost finished.

"Start with a normal stroke. When you have drawn the paddle back by the side of the boat, turn it gently and hold it in that position for a few seconds at the end. Watch which direction the canoe takes."

Chris continues, "Experiment by placing the paddle at different angles and allow the boat to follow accordingly."

"Okay," says Smith, and makes another stroke using a less extreme angle at the end this time—watching how the bow of the boat naturally reacts.

The lake is silent and pristine in the early morning light. Smith makes a few straight strokes to move the canoe forward. His paddle meets the water confidently before he turns it at the end of each stroke.

Like gently applying a brake, he thinks.

In spite of a tendency to over-steer, he manages to get the boat to veer to the left or the right as he paddles. "Hey, this is fun!"

Chris chuckles, "You'll soon be able to go out by yourself."

"Do I keep switching sides with the paddle?" asks Smith.

"With this stroke, you can paddle on one side only and still go straight."

"As soon as I get it down a little more," Smith tells him, "I'd like to try paddling the canoe by myself."

The water is mirror smooth and with each stroke, he can hear individual drops of water falling from the paddle to the lake. Out of nowhere, he blurts out, "I still don't know what to do about Seraphim."

"I suspect you've given it a lot of thought," Chris says kindly.

"I have, and it's driving me crazy. You know me, my first instinct is to hit back hard, but Seraphim is no ordinary opponent. Between us, she's kind of," he pauses, "well, nuts. There's no telling how high she would up the ante if I strike again. I might go home in a box!"

A short deep laugh escapes Chris, but Smith is so focused that he doesn't hear. He goes on passionately, "And since you pointed out the possibility of collateral damage, I can't get it out of my mind. I don't want to upset either Margaret or Chloe, especially up here."

"It's good that you're weighing the consequences of your actions."

"Yeah," says Smith, smacking the water with the flat of his paddle and causing a pair of ducks to flap awkwardly into the air with much vocal complaint. "It's not my usual style, but you got me thinking."

"I give you a lot of credit for trying," Chris tells him.

"This canoe thing seems good for me, but I have to say, Seraphim outdid herself with those Frakking little bears."

"I understand how you must feel," Chris responds patiently, "but you have to remember that Seraphim is also a P Energy State and she's used to getting her way. It takes all types to make a world, but two unbalanced P Energy State individuals don't make the best combination. Then there's the little incident of the bath oil."

"Wow, yeah," Chris exclaims. "That must really have set her off."

"Years ago," Smith tells him, "when we began our back and forth zinger thing, it seemed like fun, but yesterday when I was lost in the woods, I kind of realized that we're not teenagers playing pranks anymore. Someone could really get hurt."

Chris is quiet for so long that Smith starts to wonder if he might have offended him in some way, although he can't imagine how.

At last the older man says, "It's all about Discovering Yourself and understanding the strengths and weaknesses of your personal Energy State. You know how you get in competitive situations, especially when you are challenged."

"Yeah, I can get riled up."

"And what you're doing now is a reaction plan, and it's not working."

Birds sing from the trees around them and a fish jumps out of the water.

"I want you to remember one phrase," Chris says.

"What's that?"

"Damage Control, John. Damage Control."

"What does that mean?"

"You and your sister-in-law have a history of conflict and you knew when you agreed to come here, that it was very likely the two of you would have some kind of negative encounter."

"Sure," Smith agrees.

"Could there have been any way that you might have—not

avoided conflict with her—but at least, minimized the damage of the conflict?"

"So, is that what you mean by Damage Control?"

"Yes, but it's a little different from the usual understanding of the expression. What I'm talking about is minimizing damage before it occurs, instead of after."

"Hmm," Smith considers this. "Maybe I could have respected Margaret's wishes more and reacted less strongly." He clicks his tongue and admits, "I always jump right into the game. But you've gotta remember," he says defensively, "Seraphim made the first move!"

"On this trip she did," Chris agrees. "But how about the last several occasions on which you interacted, do you remember who did what to whom and in what order?"

"Nnno," Smith draws the word out. "Not really," he admits.

"But the probability of conflict was high," Chris points out. "If you had known in advance about the concept of Damage Control, this visit might have gone a lot more smoothly."

"Again with the Damage Control?"

Twisting around to face him, Chris says, "When everything in you is urging you to do something which you know in your heart is likely to create problems—for yourself or others—Damage Control is a safety phrase that you can draw upon."

He continues, "Damage Control means doing something that may not be the very best possible thing to do, but it's also far from the worst. It isn't exactly good, but it is the very least bad thing you can do. There are innumerable examples. For instance, if you're angry with someone, you look for an outlet for your anger that won't produce negative repercussions. It can be something simple, like going for a walk or a run—engaging in physical activity. Change your physiology, change your mind." He holds up his index finger. "You can quote me."

Smith grins, "I get it. For me, golf is a form of Damage Control. If I'm frustrated at work or having a bad day, I can take it out on that hard little white ball. I don't play my best at those times but getting out and hitting the ball around helps to clear my mind and calm my emotions."

"That's an excellent application of the principle."

He has hardly finished speaking when they hear a speedboat roaring down the lake in their direction.

"Quick, turn the canoe to face the boat," Chris tells Smith.

Paddling with all his might and twisting the blade at the end of each stroke, Smith manages to turn the long canoe around.

The Chris Craft is about 300 yards away, heading straight for them.

"Seraphim is on the attack," Chris yells. "And we can't get to the shore before she reaches us, no matter how hard we paddle."

The other boat is now 200 yards away and they can clearly see Seraphim's copper-colored curls blazing in the sun, with the high spume of the wake, like huge twin waterfalls, following the boat.

"Glad I'm a good swimmer!" exclaims Smith, "I think we're gonna get wet."

The Chris Craft is less than 100 yards away when its engine suddenly stops. The boat drifts forward and Seraphim stands up, her hands on the steering wheel.

Smith doesn't know if he's imagining it or if he really can see fire coming out of her eyes. *She is, after all, the Dragon Lady.*

Chris tells him to turn the canoe towards shore, and as the distance increases between the two boats, Smith begins to breathe normally.

"That was a close call!" he cries. "We're Frakking lucky she ran out of gas."

"Luck," Chris says quietly, "has nothing to do with it."

"Whaddaya mean?"

"After that first attack of hers on the water, I've been thinking how we might anticipate and adapt in the event of similar attack."

He holds up a square remote-control device. "I rigged her engine a few days ago so that if she tried to swamp us again, I could stop it."

Smith stares at him and bursts into laughter.

"Don't get too jolly," Chris warns. "She's not going to respond well."

"You're right," Smith agrees soberly. "But I gotta say, you sure know how to illustrate a lesson."

Together they paddle the canoe parallel to the shore, both of them breathing normally now that Seraphim's attack has been neutralized.

Chris begins, "Some of the most profound spiritual lessons are learned on the battlefield."

"Okay," Smith's face lights up, "now you've got my interest."

"There's a very famous book in India's Vedic literature,"

Chris continues, "called the *Bhagavad-Gita*. It tells the story of Arjuna, the noblest and purest warrior of his time, and Krishna, the greatest sage and spiritual luminary of any age, who was his charioteer. At the beginning of the *Gita*, Arjuna is on the battlefield, angry and eager to do battle because the people he is fighting are dishonest, deceitful, and blatantly immoral. Dedicated to fighting evil, Arjuna is compelled to do his duty and remove his enemies from power. But before the fighting begins, Krishna reminds him that the opposing army is made up of Arjuna's own relatives."

"Ah, interesting," observes Smith, "like Seraphim is mine."

Chris looks at him and goes on. "The effect on Arjuna is devastating. Torn between his duty and his natural affection for his kinsfolk, he becomes despondent. He loves his family, yet he knows that they have committed great wrongs. His heart and mind are divided. Pulled in both directions, he is in a state of inaction. His only solution is to ask Krishna for his wise advice."

Smith reflects, "I don't think that I'd ever have that problem."

"We may never face such an extreme choice involving life and death, but each day brings us challenges. We deal with misunderstandings at home and work all the time. And in every situation, we want our response to produce the best possible result for ourselves and for others. Not all our decisions will be perfect but agonizing over the right move doesn't help."

"I can sympathize with this guy Arjuna," says Smith. "Last night I agonized about what to do about Seraphim. So, tell me," he urges, "what advice does Krishna give him?"

"Krishna teaches Arjuna to transcend."

There's a pause. "Are you talking about TM?" Smith asks. "How can a person meditate when they are about to go into a battle?"

Chris's bushy white brows rise. "You're right, it's a very unusual place to learn how to meditate, but that's what Krishna did. Right there, between two armies ready to destroy each other, he teaches Arjuna how to transcend—in other words, how to practice Transcendental Meditation."

Smith's mouth opens a little but for a few seconds he says nothing. "Then what happens?" he asks with rapt attention.

"Arjuna's nervous system was so strong, so pure and refined," Chris tells him, "that a single act of transcending was all he needed to optimize his brain functioning. When he experienced that unbounded state of consciousness, he had access to a level of creation in which everything is infinitely correlated, a level of complete knowledge and infinite power."

"So, he was a superhero?"

"Much better. Every choice that Arjuna made was in tune with all the laws of nature."

"Huh, that's a really good story! I'll have to read it sometime."

"I think you'll enjoy it."

"Yeah," Smith muses, "a warrior learning to meditate in the middle of a battlefield so he can make perfect choices. Man, whoever wrote that deserves some kind of award."

Again, he is silent for a moment, then he asks if Chris plans to teach him TM right there in the canoe, before Seraphim can make her next move.

"I'm not Krishna," Chris laughs, "and you are not Arjuna. And anyway, we don't have time for that."

They turn to see another big motorboat racing towards them.

Chris says ominously. "Someone brought her a backup boat in record time."

"Come on, we have to hand it to her," Smith says, "the woman is resourceful."

Chris's face is serious, and he nods without speaking.

Smith tries to inject humor into the situation. "What do we do now, oh all-knowing teacher? I suppose there's no chance that you have a remote for this boat?"

"Nope. Now we come up with a new plan."

"But she's getting kind of close." Smith is starting to worry. "What kind of plan do have in mind?"

"There's not a moment to spare," Chris says forcefully. "Follow my lead and jump overboard!"

"You're kidding."

"I'm serious," he says with urgency. "Jump! Now! I'm going to."

Chris dives in and Smith does as he was told, more or less flopping over the side into the water as Chris's head breaks the surface.

Single-handedly, he flips the canoe over. Seraphim's new boat is less than 25 yards away, approaching at full speed.

Chris grips Smith's shoulder. "Get under the canoe," he tells him. "Don't worry, there's plenty of air."

They both sink down beside the protective shell of the craft, emerging into its elongated and surprisingly spacious interior. The ROAR of the speedboat and the whine of its engine echoes and reverberates in the cave-like enclosure as Seraphim's craft makes tight circles around them. The sides of the canoe rock violently in the waves, and pale lines of reflected light dance wildly on the wet cedar walls and across their faces.

After a few minutes of circling the upturned canoe, Seraphim must have become bored because she took off, and the sound of the big engines diminished quickly to silence. The men grin at each other.

"We got a little wet," Smith's voice resonates in the hollow space, "but at least she didn't have the satisfaction of capsizing us. I gotta say, Chris, these 'show and tell' lessons of yours knock my socks off."

Chris cackles. "Ancient masters of war say, 'When offence and retreat are both impossible, confuse the enemy in any way you can.' "

"Good one," Smith says, and uses his knuckles to wipe water from his eyes. "Now what?"

"Now we continue to adapt," Chris informs him before ducking under the side of the canoe and rising to the surface of the lake. Smith follows, and they both hold on to the side of their overturned craft.

"Some other time," Chris tells him, "we'll spend a half hour and I'll teach you how to right the canoe and empty it in the middle of the lake. Today, we're close enough to shore to just drag it in. I'll pull the bow painter and you push from the rear.

Kick like crazy."

"Aye-aye, Captain!"

CHAPTER 7 COMMENTARY

Types of Meditation

Chris reminds Smith that each choice he makes has consequences. He then explains a useful principle known as Damage Control. Any action that minimizes the potential damage of a particular choice can be considered as Damage Control. This is part of Step 6, Improve and Integrate, which involves managing the triggers in your environment.

Chris advises Smith to:

- Adapt by not reacting to Seraphim's attacks
- Make use of a technique which will help calm his mind and body

He tells the story of the *Bhagavad-Gita*, in which Arjuna learns how to meditate immediately before a battle.

In each of our other books, Smith has been advised to learn Transcendental Meditation, or TM, but he has so far procrastinated, using the excuse that he doesn't have time. Since we wrote our very first Mr. Smith book, *Quantum Golf*, in 1991, meditation has become a household word. Many businesses today have meditation rooms, and meditation apps have captured the interest of millions. In his recent research, Dr. Fred Travis clearly shows that different types of meditation produce different results.

The Three Main Categories Of Meditation Procedures and Their Effects On The Brain:

FOCUSED ATTENTION (including Zen, compassion, qigong, and vipassana) produces gamma brain waves (around 40 cycles per second), indicating that the brain is concentrated and focused

OPEN MONITORING (including mindfulness and Kriya yoga) produces theta brain waves (5 to 7 cycles per second), indicating that the mind is in a more contemplative state

AUTOMATIC SELF-TRANSCENDING (primarily Transcendental Meditation) produces coherent alpha 1 brain waves (8 to 10 cycles per second), indicating that the mind is in a unique state of restful alertness

According to Dr. Travis, meditation techniques that use Focused Attention train the mind to concentrate more closely and for longer periods. Meditation techniques that use Open Monitoring help develop greater awareness of our body, such as our breathing patterns, and help cultivate insight into our action.

Automatic Self-Transcending meditation is fundamentally different from the other two because it does not involve thinking about anything—instead, it allows the mind to settle down to a silent state while at the same time becoming more aware. The goal of Transcendental Meditation is not to develop a specific mental ability but to "transcend" to subtler levels of thinking and ultimately the source of all thought, the field of creative intelligence, so that every action becomes more powerful and successful. See Resource Materials Section 2 for more information on TM.

TROUBLE IN PARADISE

EPILOGUE

The Peace Offering

Chris, Smith, and the rest of the family are seated around a large picnic table outside Margaret's cottage. Multicolored streamers and balloons hang from overhead branches, bouncing slightly in the soft summer breeze. Seraphim is seated at the head of the table, cluttered with the remnants of a delicious lunch. Margaret sits on one side of her.

Smith had expected to be seated either beside or across from his wife, but as soon as they arrived, Seraphim had grabbed his arm and pulled him down beside her. And there he sits, having been pointedly ignored for the entire festive lunch.

He stares moodily at Chris, who is at the far end of the table. Except for Smith, everyone is talking and laughing.

Without warning, Seraphim reaches over to hold a glass container close to his face. His head turtles back reflexively on his neck and sees that there is a small brass bee perched decoratively on its lid.

Giving him a wide and temporarily restored smile, she asks, "Would you care for some honey, Smithy?"

His nostrils flair as he takes in a deep breath and counts slowly and determinedly: One one-thousand, Two one-thousand, Three one-thousand, Four one-thousand, Five one-thousand.

Aware of what is happening, Margaret stands abruptly. "Attention everyone," she says, tapping her glass with a spoon. This is apparently a signal for Chloe to come out of the cottage carrying a beautifully decorated layer cake, alight with candles. The little group sings Happy Birthday to Seraphim, who does not hide her pleasure. Quietly and unobtrusively, Smith gets up and walks over to stand up beside Chris.

"Before our dear Seraphim blows out her candles," Margaret says, "I would like to thank her for doing such a splendid job preserving the beauty and ecology of Paradise Lake. As head of the conservation committee for more than three decades, she has led the fight to keep out unwanted developers and maintain the lake's purity, ensuring the quality of life for future generations."

She raises her glass to her sister. "We thank you with all our hearts and it's our dearest wish that Paradise Lake has many more years of your invaluable stewardship. Now, Chris and my husband would both like to present you with a token of their esteem."

Seraphim's face tightens as she watches them approach. They are carrying a slender rectangular object wrapped in beautiful honeycomb pattern paper, and each wears his own version of an expression of submission and respect.

Somewhat apprehensively, she accepts the gift and unwraps it. Her face lights up. "Oh! What have you done?" Her eyes fly to her sister. "You know how much I've wanted this painting!"

As she examines each detail with appreciation, Smith leans over and whispers in her ear, "Please take this as a peace offering."

Her face softens and she whispers back, "I accept the terms of your surrender. Unconditionally."

He laughs, shaking his head, and all enmity between them is momentarily dispelled. They smile knowingly at each other, and Seraphim holds up the exquisite gift.

Chris, Chloe, and Margaret burst into applause and Smith sits down again. His wife smiles tenderly at him, squeezing his knee.

Three short days before that, however, she had not been so happy with him. In spite of his confidence that he had successfully hidden his escalating feud with her sister, Margaret had pieced the whole thing together.

The game was up the moment he had entered the cottage in wet clothes with the story of Chris capsizing the canoe. But she knew there wasn't a canoe in the world that would capsize with Chris in it—unless he wanted it to.

As her husband stood dripping in front of her, she informed him that his war with Seraphim was over.

With spectacularly unsuccessful feigned innocence, Smith asked, "What war?"

"Whatever conflict you and my sister have been engaged in since we arrived."

"Even if I wanted to end it," he protested, "and I'm not sure that I do—"

His wife's expression stopped him cold. "Of course," he said quickly, "I understand that she's your sister, and I know that I promised to try to get along with her while we're here. And… and…and…." His chest deflated with an audible rush of air that signaled complete capitulation. In a much quieter voice, he said, "Tell me what I can do to make things better, Margaret."

She reminded him that Chris was in possession of a landscape painting which Seraphim had long coveted. She had even admitted that she thought about it every day, and had never forgiven Chris.

"It is going to take something extraordinary," Margaret explained, "something quite special, to stop the fighting."

Smith burst out defensively, "Didn't know a thing about the painting!"

"I understand, but you need to recognize that she has it in for both of you."

He was flabbergasted. "Well, what the Frakk are we supposed to do?"

"Chris has agreed to give it to her for the sake of re-establishing peace at the lake and protecting its future."

Smith stood there, nonplussed. *Just like that? My battle with Seraphim is over? Not with a bang, but with a birthday present!*

Immediately, he called Chris on his cellphone and they agreed to take a short walk together to discuss Margaret's plan.

Chris told Smith that what was happening was an excellent demonstration of something called Cosmic Coherence. It was his view that "Margaret's suggestion for us to give Seraphim the painting is a brilliant way for us to create coherence."

"Us?" repeated Smith.

"Sure. We're both in hot water, why not?"

"I suppose," Smith agreed uncertainly.

"Among other things," Chris pointed out, "it will create a strong and maybe even a permanent truce among the three of us."

Smith had his doubts. "I dunno. Margaret's fond of that Biblical saying, 'Love thy enemy,' but I'm honestly not sure how long I can keep that up with Seraphim."

"There is another great truth," Chris told him. "You may be less familiar with it, but it could shine some light on the situation."

"What's that?"

"Sometimes when you lose you win."

Smith stared at him. "How the Frakk is losing winning?"

"When you lose something, there is often an even bigger picture in which you are also gaining, and also learning, something else, something more significant and lasting. It's just that we can't always see it at the time."

"Frankly Chris," he sighed, "I really really like to win, so don't think that any of this is easy for me."

"I believe you," Chris said sympathetically. "But it's a question of the larger picture. Ending your conflict now will make your family life easier and much happier in the future. It is your great fortune to have a wife who knows this, and I think that you're smart enough to listen to her."

Smith had to agree. "Yeah, I try to do that whenever I can. I've found that it saves me a whole lot of trouble."

"Another thing," Chris pointed out, "is that giving is one of the easiest ways to create coherence. And the simple act of meditating also creates coherence, affecting not only your own life but everything around you."

"I see the beauty of Margaret's plan," Smith conceded freely now. "I'm ready to capitulate!"

"That's excellent!" Chris exclaimed. "And I'm happy to celebrate this moment with you. We have faced a worthy adversary and we learned a great deal. I believe that this is the beginning of the rest of our journey together."

EPILOGUE COMMENTARY

Creating Coherence

Here, Chris explains more about how TBC Life Coaching creates coherence. We learn that there are a number of ways to create coherence, and that perhaps the simplest is by giving, which is how Margaret resolves the conflict with Seraphim. The painting is part of a celebration and makes a perfect peace offering, which creates a strong, if temporary, truce.

Meditation is a more powerful way to create coherence. Research shows that there is an improvement in all aspects of the mental and physical health of meditators. One very significant study found that people with heart disease who practiced the TM technique regularly were 48% less likely to have a heart attack or stroke, or to die from other causes, compared with a control group who simply attended a health education class. See Resource Materials Section 2.

Another way to help increase the coherence of your mind and body is by following daily recommendations from Ayurveda. See Resource Materials Section 6. And by identifying and understanding your Energy State, you can create greater coherence in your relationships and family life. See Resource Materials Sections 9 and 10.

The Coherence Code explains that coherence is the most important factor involved in making a company more successful. Dame Georgina describes coherence as a state in which there are orderly relationships between all parts of a system, and gives an example of a migrating flock of geese whose formation or shape is never static, but always in a dynamic state of order.

Coherence, she told Smith, can be seen everywhere in nature, from the growth of the smallest flower to the vast and precise rotation of the planets. She said that the top five companies in the world—Amazon, Apple, Facebook, Google, and Microsoft—all have an agile and coherent mindset, which allows them to quickly adapt to their customers' needs.

In terms of the environment, peer-reviewed studies show that the group practice of TM and its advanced techniques creates coherence in the collective consciousness of a city or country—as indicated by a reduction in violence, improved quality of life, and other reliable measures. See Resource Materials Section 11.

By the conclusion of the book, it becomes clear that Mr. Smith needs all of the coherence-creating tools that he can lay his hands on, along with every bit of Chris's wisdom and coaching skills, in order to build a set of positive habits which will ensure both the maintenance and continued improvement of his relationship with Seraphim.

SELF COACHING

Applying Total Brain Coaching to Your Life

BE YOUR OWN COACH

Self Coaching Equals Ultimate Self Empowerment is the companion book to *Trouble In Paradise*. It is a book about habit change and neuroadaptability. Most of us don't have access to a great coach to co-create our habit change journey, so we wrote this book to help you *be your own coach*.

Self Coaching is knowing who you are and how to stay in balance, be adaptable, and maximize your energy and coherence in a rapidly changing world. It is also about having a vision of who you want to be and exploring how you can best realize your goals. Essentially, Self Coaching is about fully empowering yourself.

ABOUT THE AUTHORS

DR. ROBERT KEITH WALLACE

Dr. Robert Keith Wallace did pioneering research on the Transcendental Meditation technique. His seminal papers—published in *Science*, *American Journal of Physiology*, and *Scientific American*—on a fourth major state of consciousness support a new paradigm of mind-body medicine and total brain development. Dr. Wallace is the founding President of Maharishi International University and has traveled around the world giving lectures at major universities and institutes, and has written and co-authored several books.

He is presently a Trustee of Maharishi International University, and Chairman of the Department of Physiology and Health.

SAMANTHA WALLACE

As a former model, Samantha Jones Wallace was featured on the covers of *Vogue*, *Cosmopolitan*, *Good Housekeeping*, and *Look* magazines. She is a long-time practitioner of Transcendental

Meditation and has a deep understanding of Ayurveda and its relationship to health and wellbeing. Samantha is a co-author of *Gut Crisis, The Rest And Repair Diet, The Coherence Code, Total Brain Coaching,* and *Trouble In Paradise.*

She is also the co-author of *Quantum Golf* (Editions One and Two) and was an editor of *Dharma Parenting.* Her most recent book is *Beauty, Ayurveda, and Essential Oil Skincare—A Friendly Introduction,* co-authored with Robert Keith Wallace, PhD, and Veronica Wells Butler, M.D.

Happily married for over forty years, the Wallaces have a combined family of four children and six grandchildren.

TED WALLACE

Ted Wallace is currently an Agile Coach at Principal Financial Group. He has completed two Master of Science degrees, one in Computer Science and the other in Physiology, from Maharishi International University. He is a certified Scrum Master Professional (CSM, CSPO, CSP, CTC) and a registered corporate coach (RCC) with thousands of hours of coaching sessions.

ACKNOWLEDGMENTS

We would like to thank our talented friend George Foster for his wonderful cover design. We also thank Fran Clark for proofreading.

TROUBLE IN PARADISE

RESOURCE MATERIALS

12 SECTIONS

SECTION 1

Energy State Characteristics

V ENERGY STATE

V Energy State individuals are bright, good at creating new ideas and projects, and able to learn quickly. If, however, they become imbalanced, they may easily lose their energy and can become fatigued and oversensitive. They may also experience mood swings, and they will then have difficulty in following a project through to the end. The secret for a V person to maintain balance is to follow a good routine. Certain simple dietary and lifestyle changes will also greatly help to rebalance and sustain a V Energy State person.

P ENERGY STATE

P Energy State individuals tend to be well-organized and purposeful. They often possess good energy and a strong and penetrating intellect, and can be good leaders. It is no coincidence that businesspeople and athletes are frequently P individuals. When a P is imbalanced, they may have trouble controlling their anger, or, at the very least, irritation, from time to time. They can also be impatient, difficult to interact with, and controlling. The key to a P keeping in good balance is for them to eat on time and not become overheated. *It's that simple!*

K ENERGY STATE

K Energy State people tend to be steady and take some time to carefully consider any decision. They are not easily upset, and are often easygoing and agreeable. If they go out of balance, however, they can become stubborn and seem to lack ambition. The key to keeping a K person in good balance is to keep them physically active and mentally stimulated.

VP and PV ENERGY STATES

A VP Energy State person is similar to a PV Energy State, but in written form, whichever Energy State is listed first is the one that predominates. A VP person is quick, inspiring, and full of new ideas, but at the same time is also focused and ready to complete the project. VPs can be both energetic and sensitive. One part of them is in motion, while the other is steadily goal-oriented.

When VPs are in good balance, they draw energy from their P qualities. When they are out of balance, their V qualities can cause them to become over-stimulated and quickly exhausted. This duality produces a reasonably strong but variable energy.

The digestion of a VP is like their energy, good but variable, and their appetite is similar. Because their gut is partially V, they may be a discriminating eater with strong preferences, and can be hungry one minute and not interested in food the next. But because their gut is also partially P, they need ample meals to sustain physical and mental activity. The presence of P indicates that it is especially important for VP individuals to eat on time. As a combination type, they have a more balanced appetite than people with either a pure V or a pure P Energy State.

When VPs are in good balance, they rarely have digestive problems. When out of balance, however, digestive issues can range from weak digestion to hyperacidity.

VP Energy State people are agile and have good energy and strength. They may also tend to be graceful. VP Energy individuals do not have a problem falling asleep unless they are over-stimulated before going to bed.

VK or KV ENERGY STATE

This Energy State is an interesting combination of opposites. The V Energy State is light and airy, while the K Energy State is heavy and earthy. This combination indicates both steadiness and enthusiasm.

When VK is in good balance, the result is good health and physical stamina. When it is out of balance, VK people are prone to frequent colds and respiratory problems. With this particular energy state, it's important to remember that an imbalance of V will always push K out of balance, so V imbalances need to be addressed as soon as possible. VKs don't do well in cold or damp weather and need to stay warm to avoid illness.

The VK combination gives rise to individuals who have a wide range of emotions. They are quick, inspiring, and full of new ideas, but at the same time they are stable, well liked, and methodical. VKs can be both grounded and sensitive. One part of them is in constant airy motion, while the other is steady and grounded.

When out of balance, a VK person tends to be spacey, withdrawn, or even depressed. They may also obsess on issues and become attached and/or anxious. It's especially good for VKs to have enjoyable social outings and to stay rested, as well as energized, in order to balance the best aspects of their mind, body, and emotions.

The digestion of a VK Energy State person is virtually the same as a KV Energy State person. Again, as we mentioned, the energy state listed first indicates which is predominant. VKs are generally strong and steady, and enjoy an occasional snack. The V part of the VK combination makes the person a grazer, with a constantly changing appetite, while their K part makes them love to eat. When they are in good balance, V and K complement each other very well. They enjoy food, but don't gain as much weight as pure K types until later in life.

When out of balance, the VK, KV digestion slows down and they become more sensitive to what they eat.

In regard to exercise, VK Energy State individuals are a mixture of opposites and may be sprinters as well as endurance runners.

VK Energy individuals can fall asleep and stay asleep as long as their V Energy State is balanced.

PK OR KP ENERGY STATE

PK Energy State people have the hot, transformative qualities of a P Energy State *plus* the cool, stable qualities of a K Energy State. If they are unable to stay in balance, however, they can boil over. PKs are generally large and strong and do well in sports. Many professional athletes are PK. They might not be the stars of the team, but they have the constitution to be very good players.

A PK tends to be strong, sturdy, content, and easygoing. Their high energy drive is steadied by their calm, easygoing nature. Imbalances can cause impatience, anger, and lethargy. They may also become argumentative, stubborn, and withdrawn. It's very important for a PK particularly to maintain healthy family relationships and friendships in order to stay in good balance.

In the heat of the moment a PK might not think problems through completely. And if decisions backfire, they may be prone to useless regret. A PK individual will be happier and healthier spending more time listening and less time making assumptions and running scenarios in their head.

The PK digestion and appetite is virtually the same as KP. In both cases, each of the combined energy states is strong, but P will predominate. People with a P gut have a good appetite, and strong digestion. If they have a PK gut, they will have an even stronger appetite. PKs like to eat, and generally digest easily. Because their gut is part K, however, their metabolism slows down at times and they may have a hard time digesting greasy foods. It's easy for PKs to gain a few extra pounds, but they can usually lose them without great effort.

When PKs are in good balance, they rarely have digestive problems. When out of balance, however, they must be aware of slower digestion and hyperacidity.

PKs need to exercise daily. They have excellent stamina in activity, but must remember not to get overheated. The PK or KP individual generally falls asleep easily and gets a good sound sleep.

VPK ENERGY STATE OR "TRI-ENERGY STATE"

This is a relatively rare mixture of the three types and, when it is in balance, shows the best qualities of each. VPKs are often creative, motivated, steady, and good-natured. When they are in good balance, they tend to be in tune with their body and emotions and may be intuitive. Physically strong with a moderate build, VPKs are usually in good health. They avoid most seasonal illnesses and experience only mild to moderate symptoms during each season (e.g. dry skin in the winter, some lethargy in the spring, and mild heat intolerance in the summer).

Life for a VPK becomes complicated when one or more of their three Energy States goes out of balance and it is helpful for them to learn to "check in" with themselves and be alert to when something doesn't feel right. The best advice for VPKs is to treat any imbalances in the following order:

- Start by balancing V
- Go on to balance P
- Finally address K

Keep in mind that it takes a VPK Energy State person longer to come back into balance than the other Energy State combinations.

The digestion and appetite of a VPK Energy State person should be good since they have a stronger digestion than others. They can eat almost any kind of food and rarely experience excessive hunger or thirst. However, because their symptoms are usually mild and somewhat veiled, it is hard to pinpoint how and when they go out of balance, so it's especially valuable for them to learn to listen to their body and use Self Pulse as a reliable indicator of their state of balance.

Possessing all three characteristics, they are capable of different types of exercise. The main thing is to not overdo it. Because of their K Energy State, sleep is their friend. If they do go out of balance, it is usually the V Energy State which causes a sleep problem.

ENERGY STATE CONCLUSION

No single Energy State is better than another and each of us can rise to our full potential by staying in balance and achieving maximum levels of energy, performance, and success. For recommendations about specific Energy State diets, including teas, spice mixes, and recipes, see *The Rest and Repair Diet: Heal Your Gut, Improve Your Physical and Mental Health, and Lose Weight*, and visit the website at docgut.com.

SCIENTIFIC RESEARCH ON AYURVEDA AND ENERGY STATES

Recent studies have shown that there is a scientific basis to Ayurveda and its evaluation of each person's Energy State or

Prakriti. There is a whole new field emerging called Ayurgenomics. Genetic research, for example, has shown that the Vata (V Energy State), Pitta (P Energy State), and Kapha (K Energy State) Prakriti each expresses a different set of genes. See scientific references 1 and 2 in the list below.

Genes in the immune response pathways, for example, were turned on or up-regulated in extreme Pittas. In Vatas, genes related to cell cycles were turned on. In Kaphas it was found that genes in the immune signaling pathways were turned on. Inflammatory genes were up-regulated in Vatas, whereas up-regulation of oxidative stress pathway genes was observed in Pittas and Kaphas. See reference number 3 below. CD25 (activated B cells) and CD56 (natural killer cells) were higher in Kaphas. CYP2C19 genotypes, a family of genes that help in detoxification and metabolism of certain drugs, were turned off or down-regulated in Kapha types and turned on in Pitta types. See references 4 and 5 below.

Extreme Vata, Pitta, and Kapha individuals also have significant differences in specific physiological measurements. Again, see references 1 and 2 below. Triglycerides, total cholesterol, high low-density lipoprotein (LDL), and low high-density lipoprotein (HDL) concentrations—all common risk factors for cardiovascular disease—were reported to be higher in Kaphas compared to Vatas. Hemoglobin and red blood cell count were higher in Pittas compared to others. Serum prolactin was higher in Vata individuals. See reference 2 below. High levels of triglyceride,

VLDL and LDL levels and lower levels of HDL cholesterol distinguish Kaphas from others. See reference 6 below.

Adenosine diphosphate-induced maximal platelet aggregation was the highest among Vata/Pitta types. See reference 7 below. In diabetic patients, there were significant decreases in systolic blood pressure in Vata/Pitta, Pitta/Kapha, and Vata/Kapha types after walking (isotonic exercise). The Vata/Pitta types also showed significant decreases in mean diastolic blood pressure. See reference 8 below. In terms of biochemistry, Kaphas had elevated digoxin levels, increased free radical production, and reduced scavenging, increased tryptophan catabolites and reduced tyrosine catabolites, increased glycoconjugate levels, and increased cholesterol. Pittas showed the opposite biochemical patterns. Vatas showed normal biochemical patterns. See reference 9 below.

A study of basic cardiovascular responses reported that heart rate variability and arterial blood pressure during specific postural changes, exercise, and cold pressor test did not vary with constitutional type. See reference 10 below. A more recent paper measuring cold pressor test, standing-to-lying ratio, and pupillary responses in light and dark reported that Kapha types have higher parasympathetic activity and lower sympathetic activity in terms of cardiovascular reactivity as compared to Pitta or Vata types. See reference 11 below.

A recent study also showed that predominantly Vata, Pitta, or

Kapha people had a different composition of bacteria in their microbiome. See reference 12 below. Finally, Travis and Wallace have reviewed many of these findings, and created a neurophysiological model of Vata, Pitta, and Kapha based on the functioning of different neural networks. See reference 13 below.

REFERENCES

1. Dey S, Pahwa P. Prakriti and its associations with metabolism, chronic diseases, and genotypes: Possibilities of new born screening and a lifetime of personalized prevention. *J Ayurveda Integr Med* 2014;5:15-24.

2. Wallace, R.K. Ayurgenomics and Modern Medicine. Medicina 2020, 56, 661.

3. Juyal RC, Negi S, Wakhode P, Bhat S, Bhat B, Thelma BK. Potential of ayurgenomics approach in complex trait research: Leads from a pilot study on rheumatoid arthritis. *PLoS One.* 2012;7:e45752.

4. Ghodke Y, Joshi K, Patwardhan B. Traditional medicine to modern pharmacogenomics: Ayurveda Prakriti type and CYP2C19 gene polymorphism associated with the metabolic variability. *Evid Based Complement Alternat Med* 2011;2011:249528.

5. Aggarwal S, Negi S, Jha P, Singh PK, Stobdan T, Pasha MA. Indian genome variation consortium. EGLN1 involvement in high-altitude adaptation revealed through genetic analysis of extreme constitution types defined in Ayurveda. *Proc Natl Acad Sci* 2010;107:18961-6.

6. Mahalle NP, Kulkarni MV, Pendse NM, Naik SS. Association of constitutional type of Ayurveda with cardiovascular risk factors,

inflammatory markers and insulin resistance. *J Ayurveda Integr Med* 2012;3:150-7.

7. Bhalerao S, Deshpande T, Thatte U. Prakriti (Ayurvedic concept of constitution) and variations in Platelet aggregation. *BMC Complement Altern Med* 2012;12:248-56.

8. Tiwari S, Gehlot S, Tiwari SK, Singh G. Effect of walking (aerobic isotonic exercise) on physiological variants with special reference to Prameha (diabetes mellitus) as per Prakriti. *Ayu* 2012;33:44-9.

9. Kurup RK, Kurup PA. Hypothalamic digoxin, hemispheric chemical dominance, and the tridosha theory. *Int J Neurosci* 2003;113:657-81.

10. Tripathi PK, Patwardhan K, Singh G. The basic cardiovascular responses to postural changes, exercise and cold pressor test: Do they vary in accordance with the dual constitutional types of Ayurveda? *Evid Based Complement Alternat Med* 2011;201:251-9.

11. Rapolu SB, Kumar M, Singh G, Patwardhan K. Physiological variations in the autonomic responses may be related to the constitutional types defined in Ayurveda. *J Humanitas Med* 2015;5:e7.

12. Chauhan NS, Pandey R, Mondal AK, Gupta S, Verma MK, Jain S, et al. Western Indian Rural Gut Microbial Diversity in Extreme Prakriti Endo-Phenotypes Reveals Signature Microbes. *Front. Microbiol.* 2018; 9:118. doi: 10.3389/fmicb.2018.00118. eCollection 2018.

13. Travis, FT, Wallace, RK, Dosha brain-types: A neural model of individual differences. *J Ayurveda Integr Med*. 2015; 6, 280-85.

SECTION 2

Meditation

THE TRANSCENDENTAL MEDITATION PROGRAM

The Transcendental Meditation technique is a unique, simple, and effective mental procedure. It takes about twenty minutes, twice each day, in which you sit comfortably with your eyes closed. It involves no belief or philosophy, no mood or lifestyle. Most people begin the technique for practical reasons, such as a desire for more energy or to decrease tension and anxiety. Over ten million people of all ages, cultures, and religions have learned TM.

TM uses the natural tendency of the mind to spontaneously experience states of greater and greater happiness. The technique involves a real and measurable process of physiological refinement that utilizes the inherent capacity of the nervous system to refine its own functioning and unfold its full potential. During TM practice, your attention is very naturally and spontaneously drawn to quieter, more orderly states of mental activity until all mental activity is transcended, and you are left with no thoughts or sensations, only the experience of pure awareness itself. The result of the regular practice of TM is that your entire nervous system becomes rejuvenated and revitalized, and you become more successful and fulfilled in activity.

Extensive research documents the effectiveness of TM in improving both physical and mental health. TM produces a unique state of restful alertness (1-3) with different brain wave patterns from other techniques of meditation (4). The practice of this technique helps every area of life by removing stress from the nervous system. Over 600 studies at more than 200 research institutes and universities have been conducted on the Transcendental Meditation program, and more than 380 of these studies have been published in peer-reviewed journals. [Note to Reader: "Peer-reviewed" means that scientists, whose qualifications and competencies are on a similar level of accomplishment as those of the authors of the study, have evaluated the work. This method is the gold standard of science, employed to maintain the highest standard of quality and credibility.]

The US National Institutes of Health has awarded over $25 million to study the effects of TM on health, particularly on heart disease, the #1 killer in the US. It is particularly interesting to note that researchers who conducted an important study at the

Medical College of Wisconsin in Milwaukee reported that the more regularly the patients meditated, the longer was their term of survival (5).

A number of important studies have shown that TM reduces high blood pressure (6). A statement from the American Heart Association concluded:

> The Transcendental Meditation technique is the only meditation practice that has been shown to lower blood pressure.
>
> Because of many negative studies or mixed results and a paucity of available trials, all other meditation techniques (including MBSR) received a 'Class III, no benefit, Level of Evidence C' recommendation. Thus, other meditation techniques are not recommended in clinical practice to lower BP at this time.
>
> Transcendental Meditation practice is recommended for consideration in treatment plans for all individuals with blood pressure > 120/80 mm Hg.
>
> Lower blood pressure through Transcendental Meditation practice is also associated with substantially reduced rates of death, heart attack, and stroke (7).

Research shows that TM practice reduces cholesterol levels (8). Studies also show that meditators exhibit an improved ability to adapt to stressful situations (9,10) and a marked decrease in levels of plasma cortisol, commonly known as the "stress hormone" (11).

Research results in various areas of health document improvements in such conditions as asthma, diabetes, metabolic syndrome, pain, alcohol and drug abuse, and mental health (12-17). In a five-year study on some 2000 individuals, researchers showed that TM meditators used medical and surgical health care services approximately one-half as often as did other insurance users. This study was conducted in cooperation with Blue Cross Blue Shield and controlled for other factors that might affect health care use, such as cost sharing, age, gender, geographic distribution, and profession. The TM subjects also showed a far lower rate of increase in health care utilization with increasing age (18).

In Québec, Canada, researchers compared the changes in physician costs for TM practitioners with those of non-practitioners over a five-year period. This study is particularly reliable because the Canadian government tracked health care costs closely for both meditators and the control group, due to Canada's national health care system. After the first year, the health care costs of the TM group decreased 11%, and after five years, their cumulative cost reduction was 28%. TM patients required fewer referrals, resulting in lower medical expenses for prescription drugs, tests, hospitalization, surgery, and other treatments (19).

Studies have documented how TM can slow and even reverse the aging process. One study showed that long-term TM meditators had a biological age roughly twelve years younger than their non-meditating counterparts (20). Researchers at Harvard University studied the effects of TM on mental health, behavioral flexibility, blood pressure, and longevity, in residents of homes for the elderly. The subjects were randomly assigned either to a no-treatment group or to one of three treatment programs: the TM program, mindfulness training, or a relaxation program. Initially, all three groups were similar on pretest measures and expectancy of benefits, yet after only three months, the TM group showed significant improvements in cognitive functioning and blood pressure compared to the control groups. Reports from the TM subjects, compared to those of the mindfulness or the relaxation subjects, indicated that the TM practitioners felt more absorbed during their practice, and better and more relaxed immediately afterward. Overall, more TM subjects found their practice to be personally valuable than members of either of the control groups (21).

The most striking finding is that TM practice not only reverses age-related declines in overall health, but also directly enhances longevity. All the members of the TM group were still alive three years after the program began, in contrast to about only half of the members of the control groups. Research on the Transcendental Meditation program clearly shows that growing old no longer need signify a loss in the quality of life; rather, it can be an opportunity for further development (22-23). Scientists have suggested that one of the ways TM may improve health and increase longevity is by changing the expression of specific beneficial genes in our DNA (24-25).

Long-term changes in brain functioning have also been correlated with decreased stress-reactivity and neuroticism, and increased self-development, intelligence, learning ability, and self-actualization (26-30). One important psychological study on TM shows a significant decrease in levels of anxiety in TM practitioners as compared to subjects practicing other relaxation techniques (31). Studies in a variety of work and business settings show significantly increased productivity and efficiency (32,33).

TM is learned from a qualified TM teacher, and is taught in 7 steps, usually within a week's time according to your schedule. Most of the steps take 1-2 hours (though some are shorter). There is also a brief but important follow-up meeting 10 days after you learn the practice, and then once a month for the first three months after your TM course. All of these meetings are included in the course fee, along with lifelong support for your meditation program, including individual meditation checking, advanced meetings, and other special events.

Although there are a number of advanced TM programs, TM is always the core technique and will continue to benefit your life whether you choose to take an advanced program or not. (For more information on how to start TM, see TM.org.)

SELECTED REFERENCES

1. Wallace RK. Physiological effects of Transcendental Meditation. *Science* 167:1751-1754, 1970

2. Wallace RK, et al. A wakeful hypometabolic physiologic state. *American Journal of Physiology* 221(3): 795-799, 1971

3. Wallace RK. Physiological effects of the Transcendental Meditation technique: A proposed fourth major state of consciousness. Ph.D. thesis. Physiology Department, University of California, Los Angeles, 1970

4. Travis FT and Shear J. Focused attention, open monitoring and automatic self-transcending: Categories to organize meditations from Vedic, Buddhist and Chinese traditions. *Consciousness and Cognition* 19(4):1110-1118, 2010

5. Schneider RH, et al. Stress Reduction in the Secondary Prevention of Cardiovascular Disease: Randomized, Controlled Trial of Transcendental Meditation and Health Education in Blacks. *Circ Cardiovasc Qual Outcomes* 5:750-758, 2012

6. Rainforth MV, et al. Stress reduction programs in patients with elevated blood pressure: a systematic review and meta-analysis. *Current Hypertension Reports* 9:520–528, 2007

7. Brook RD, et al., Beyond Medications and Diet: Alternative Approaches to Lowering Blood Pressure. A Scientific Statement from the American Heart Association. *Hypertension* 61(6):1360-83, 2013

8. Cooper MJ, et al. Transcendental Meditation in the management of hypercholesterolemia. *Journal of Human Stress* 5(4): 24–27, 1979

9. Orme-Johnson DW and Walton KW. All approaches of preventing

or reversing effects of stress are not the same. *American Journal of Health Promotion* 12:297-299, 1998

10. Barnes VA, et al. Impact of Transcendental Meditation on cardiovascular function at rest and during acute stress in adolescents with high normal blood pressure. *Journal of Psychosomatic Research* 51: 597-605, 2001

11. Jevning R, et al. Adrenocortical activity during meditation. *Hormonal Behavior* 10(1):54-60, 1978

12. Wilson AF, et al. Transcendental Meditation and asthma. *Respiration* 32:74-80, 1975

13. Paul-Labrador M, et al. Effects of randomized controlled trial of Transcendental Meditation on components of the metabolic syndrome in subjects with coronary heart disease. *Archives of Internal Medicine* 166:1218-1224, 2006

14. Royer A. The role of the Transcendental Meditation technique in promoting smoking cessation: A longitudinal study. *Alcoholism Treatment Quarterly* 11: 219-236, 1994

15. Haratani T, et al. Effects of Transcendental Meditation (TM) on the mental health of industrial workers. *Japanese Journal of Industrial Health* 32: 656, 1990

16. Orme-Johnson DW, et al. Neuroimaging of meditation's effect on brain reactivity to pain. *NeuroReport* 17(12):1359-63, 2006

17. Alexander CN, et al. Treating and preventing alcohol, nicotine, and drug abuse through Transcendental Meditation: A review and statistical meta-analysis. *Alcoholism Treatment Quarterly* 11: 13-87, 1994.

18. Orme-Johnson DW, Herron R.E. An Innovative Approach to

Reducing Medical Care Utilization and Expenditures. *American Journal of Managed Care* 3: 135–144, 1997

19. Herron RE. Can the Transcendental Meditation Program Reduce the Medical Expenditures of Older People? A Longitudinal Cost-Reduction Study in Canada. *Journal of Social Behavior and Personality* 17(1): 415–442, 2005

20.. Wallace RK, et al. The effects of the Transcendental Meditation and TM-Sidhi program on the aging process. *International Journal of Neuroscience* 16: 53-58, 1982

21. Alexander CN, et al. Transcendental Meditation, mindfulness, and longevity. *Journal of Personality and Social Psychology* 57: 950-964, 1989

22. Alexander CN, et al. The effects of Transcendental Meditation compared to other methods of relaxation in reducing risk factors, morbidity, and mortality. *Homeostasis* 35: 243-264, 1994

23. Schneider RH, et al. Long-term effects of stress reduction on mortality in persons > 55 years of age with systemic hypertension. *American Journal of Cardiology* 95: 1060-1064, 2005

24. Duraimani S, et al. Effects of Lifestyle Modification on Telomerase Gene Expression in Hypertensive Patients: A Pilot Trial of Stress Reduction and Health Education Programs in African Americans. *PLOS ONE* 10(11): e0142689, 2015

25. Wenuganen S. Anti-Aging Effects of the Transcendental Meditation Program: Analysis of Ojas Level and Global Gene Expression. Maharishi University of Management, ProQuest Dissertations Publishing, 3630467, 2014

26. Chandler HM, et al. Transcendental Meditation and

postconventional self-development: A 10-year longitudinal study. *Journal of Social Behavior and Personality* 17(1): 93–121, 2005

27. Cranson RW, et al. Transcendental Meditation and improved performance on intelligence-related measures: A longitudinal study. *Personality and Individual Differences* 12: 1105-1116, 1991

28. So KT, and Orme-Johnson DW. Three randomized experiments on the longitudinal effects of the Transcendental Meditation technique on cognition. *Intelligence* 29: 419-440, 2001

29. Tjoa A. Increased intelligence and reduced neuroticism through the Transcendental Meditation program. *Gedrag: Tijdschrift voor Psychologie* 3: 167-182, 1975

30. Alexander CN., et al. Transcendental Meditation, self-actualization, and psychological health: A conceptual overview and statistical meta-analysis. *Journal of Social Behavior and Personality* 6: 189-247, 1991

31. Eppley KR, et al. Differential effects of relaxation techniques on trait anxiety: A meta-analysis. *Journal of Clinical Psychology* 45: 957-974, 1989

32. Alexander CN, et al. Effects of the Transcendental Meditation program on stress-reduction, health, and employee development: A prospective study in two occupational settings. *Stress, Anxiety and Coping* 6: 245–262, 1993

33. Harung HS, et al. Peak performance and higher states of consciousness: A study of world-class performers. *Journal of Managerial Psychology* 11(4): 3–23, 1996

34. Nidich S, et al. Non-trauma-focused meditation versus exposure therapy in veterans with post-traumatic stress disorder: a randomised

controlled trial. *Lancet Psychiatry.* 2018 Dec;5(12):975-986. doi: 10.1016/S2215-0366(18)30384-5. Epub 2018 Nov 15. PMID: 30449712.

SECTION 3

Gut-Brain Axis

The gut-brain axis consists of the nervous system, endocrine system, immune system, the special nervous system of the gut called the enteric nervous system, and the gut bacteria—often referred to as the gut microbiome. The composition of your gut bacteria is one of the most important factors for health.

The microbiome consists of all of the microorganisms in your body, and the largest quantity of these microscopic creatures are the 30 trillion bacteria in your gut, which have the ability to influence your brain and other parts of your physiology. Recently published scientific papers suggest that gut bacteria may be involved in numerous diseases from auto-immune disorders to heart disease. There are even studies which show that gut bacteria can influence how stress affects your state of mind, and determines whether you are happy, sad, or depressed. A new category of drugs, called Psychobiotics, consists of probiotics (or friendly bacteria) that can help improve mental health.

Certainly, you already know that it would be better for you to eat a healthier diet, but talking about it and actually doing it are separate realities. And should you follow a Paleo diet or the Mediterranean diet? There are a lot of choices and they often compete with each other. America is in the middle of the Diet Wars, with every doctor and health expert claiming that they have the solution to a healthier, longer life.

In *Gut Crisis* and *The Rest and Repair Diet* we give guidelines and specific tools to help heal your digestion and gut health. The primary emphasis of this diet is to detox and heal the digestive tract and improve your digestion by rebooting the microbiome. Personalizing your diet and lifestyle according to your Energy State will improve your physical and mental health and help you gain energy.

SECTION 4

Self Pulse

Because your cardiovascular system extends throughout your body, from your eyeballs to your liver to the joints of your big toe, it carries a wealth of information about how your physiology is functioning. Ayurvedic physicians are trained to "read" and decode this information by simply touching the pulse in your wrist with three fingers. In this way they are able to assess balances and imbalances, and even detect disease. When you learn a simplified method of Self Pulse assessment, you will be able to keep track of the amount of balance or imbalance of your Energy State or States.

Let's start with some main points:

It's very important to note that women always feel the pulse which beats in their left wrist, while men feel the pulse in the right wrist.

A woman uses the fingertips of her right hand to feel her left wrist.

A man uses the fingertips of his left hand to feel his right wrist. When we talk about the fingers and the hand, we are referring to a woman's right hand, or a man's left hand.

The styloid process is a bony projection located about a finger's width below the base of your thumb. Use the index finger of your other hand to feel it sticking out: This is the reference point for placing your fingers.

To take your own pulse, extend your arm out in front of you—right arm for men, left for women—in a comfortable position, slightly bent at the elbow, with your palm facing up. Now wrap your other hand around your wrist from behind. You are cradling the back of your wrist in the palm of your other hand. Now curl the middle three fingers—index, middle, and ring fingers—over the top of your wrist.

Position your index finger below the prominent bony bump of the styloid process, so that it's just beside the edge of the rise of this bone.

Now line up your middle and ring fingers below your index finger so the three are touching each other easily side by side. And make sure the three fingers are completely level; raise your thumb and little finger slightly so they're not touching your wrist. This is the position your fingers will always be in when you take your pulse.

Continue to slide your three fingers over and down your wrist about a quarter of an inch. Now you are ready to feel your pulse: using your fingertips, very gently press all three fingers down until you can feel the pulse beating along the radial artery. It's important to use all three fingers together and make sure that your three fingertips are approximately level, sitting in a nice line at the same level of the pulse. When you can feel the beat of your pulse in any one, or all, of your fingertips, you will have reached the first stage of pulse reading.

Each of your three fingers corresponds to one of the three main Energy States: the index finger for V Energy State or Vata; the middle finger for P Energy State or Pitta; the ring finger for K Energy State or Kapha. (Kapha may be so relaxed, or there may be so little Kapha, that it might be hard to feel it at all.)

Feel the pulse beneath each finger. (It can help to close your eyes.) Which finger feels the strongest pulse? For example, if you feel it most strongly under your middle finger, that indicates that the P Energy State is strong.

You may or may not feel a pulsation beneath all three fingertips—this is perfectly normal. In fact, most people feel their pulse under one or two fingers; only a few feel it under all three. If you're predominately a V Energy State person, for example, the pulse under your index finger will be strong. You may feel little or nothing under the other two fingers. This doesn't necessarily mean that you are imbalanced—it does means that at this time, your physiology has less P fire or K solidity in it.

What is the quality of your pulse? If it feels clear and the impulses seem coordinated—if it feels good to you overall—this indicates that your physiology is in good balance. If your pulse feels ragged or disconnected, with some impulses very weak while others are very pronounced, this tells you that you probably want to start getting yourself back in balance.

For example, you may feel that the P Energy State or Pitta area is pulsating very strongly under your index finger, which indicates that your P Energy State is too strong and has invaded the V Energy State or Vata territory. If this is the case, then it's time to stay cool and eat on time—not at your favorite spicy Mexican restaurant.

If the pulse under your ring finger feels quick and irregular, you need to get your V Energy State in better balance. Slow down, stay out of the cold wind, and stick to a regular routine.

If your K Energy State or Kapha feels very strong and dense under your middle finger, you may find that your digestion is sluggish and your mind is a bit dull. Try to balance your aggravated K Energy State with some physical activity and cut out "heavy" foods such as rich desserts and mashed potatoes.

SECTION 5

Habit Change

There are a number of best-selling books on how to change your habits. Two of the most successful are *The Power of Habit* by Charles Duhigg and *Triggers* by Marshall Goldsmith. *Tiny Habits* by BJ Fogg and *Atomic Habits* by James Clear are also excellent and both emphasize the importance of starting small, which is also recommended by Ayurveda. So, begin by picking a new habit which will be easy for you. It is also helpful if you add your new habit to one that is already established (habit stacking).

Tiny Habits uses an interesting formula: Behavior Equals Motivation x Ability x Prompt. Fogg says that the best chance you have of starting and maintaining a new habit is when both your motivation and your ability are high. He gives an example of "Katie," who likes to prepare for the following day by leaving everything neat and orderly in her work environment before going home each day. She has what he calls high motivation and high ability since it takes her less than 3 minutes to do it. She also has a prompt or cue, which is the time, 5 o'clock, every day when she stops her work and gets ready to go home.

Fogg gives an example of Katie having a hard time adopting a new habit of an early morning workout. She is trying to use her phone's alarm as a prompt, but the problem is that as soon as the alarm rings she wants to scroll through her phone and gets caught up in looking at her Facebook posts. By the time she's finished, she has no time left to exercise. With Fogg as her coach, she decided to leave her phone in the kitchen and use an alarm clock by her bed. This kind of practical solution is frequently offered by habit change experts: Change the environment, change the habit. In this case, by removing the phone and creating a new prompt, Katie changed her environment and made it easier for her to start her morning workout program.

Fogg uses what he calls Focus Mapping to help develop a new habit plan. This is similar to our program of creating a Habit Map and Habit Plan. As we have described, you write your main intention in the center of a page, add all your ideas for habit changes around it, prioritize them, and pick the best one. "I want to lose weight," for example, might be the main goal. Around it you add everything from exercising more, to eating less. You add whatever comes to your mind. Then you start to eliminate the less useful ideas and focus on one main habit which seems easy for you to adopt.

One of the most important parts of creating a Habit Plan is to make sure that your intentions are clear. If you have two conflicting intentions competing with each other, it will be harder for you to come up with a successful plan.

What Fogg and other habit change experts are missing from their habit change programs is the ability to know the unique characteristics and tendencies of each individual. Knowing your Energy State gives you an advantage because you can pick choices for habit change that fit your own particular nature. If you are a P Energy State, you know that you can stick to a discipline plan with clear intentions. If you are a V Energy State, you know it can be easy for you to become distracted with a lot of choices, so you might want to ask a P friend to be with you while you make your Habit Map and Plan. And it may be good for either a P or K friend to check in with you each day to help keep you focused. If you are a K Energy State person, you may do well with help from a P Energy State friend to help you start the process.

Another important consideration is that right before you start your habit change plan, make sure your Energy State is in balance. Again, this is a unique feature of Total Brain Coaching. It takes energy to make the change, and if you are in an imbalanced state you won't have that energy or focus. Finally, as part of being in balance, get an evaluation of your gut health. Believe it or not, your diet and digestion affect both your energy level and your state of mind.

SECTION 6

Lifestyle Guidelines

DIGESTION

- Food is medicine

- Digestion is critical for every aspect of your health

- Eat your main meal at noon when the digestive power is strongest according to Ayurveda

- Before, during, and after a meal, AVOID COLD WATER and especially ice because cold liquids reduces the fire of digestion

- Sip small amounts of room temperature or warm water with your meal instead.

- Warm water with a squeeze of lemon is not only tasty

but will help your digestion

- Always sit when you eat

- Avoid stimulation, such as the TV, telephone, or heated emotional conversations at the table

- Remaining seated for about five minutes after you have finished eating will help your digestion. This sounds strange and may feel peculiar at first, but after a while you may get to like it

- Take enough time to digest one meal before starting the next

- The freshness and purity of food is important. It is better to eat organic food than to ingest toxins, such as manmade pesticides and fertilizers

- Probiotics can be helpful and have been shown to reduce symptoms of IBS

- Discover your own Energy State and learn which foods and spices are best for you according to Ayurveda

- Periodically use *The Rest and Repair Diet* to improve your gut health and reboot your microbiome

DAILY ROUTINE

(A SIMPLE VERSION)

- Get up early and drink 8 ounces of water. The water shouldn't be cold. You can leave a covered glass of water by your bedside overnight and drink it first thing in the morning

- Reduce stress through the practice of meditation. We recommend the twice-daily practice of the Transcendental Meditation technique

- Exercise according to your Energy State, and practice yoga regularly

- Go to bed well before 10:00 pm and get enough sleep each night

YOGA

Yoga has long been recognized as a method to improve and maintain your body while you are on the path to health, happiness, success, fulfillment, and ultimately enlightenment. Research has shown that yoga postures improve certain psychological conditions, including anxiety and depression, and provide health benefits for those with high blood pressure, various pain syndromes, and immune disorders.

Choose whichever form of yoga best suits your individual nature, age, and needs. We recommend the Maharishi Yoga Asana program because it is especially respectful of your body and consciousness, and supports the experience of transcendence.

THE CYCLES OF LIFE and SUCCESSFUL AGING

According to Ayurveda, there are three main stages of life, which are based on the three doshas (also known as nature or Energy States—Vata, Pitta, and Kapha, or V, P, and K). During the first part of the lives of all children, the Kapha quality predominates regardless of one's individual nature. This is good for growth and gives a sense of contentment and happiness. If the childhood situation isn't very good, the Kapha time of life can often serve as a sort of cushion to help them get through the tough times.

As we grow out of childhood, we enter the middle, Pitta or P, stage of life. This is a more capable and responsible time, when we accomplish bigger things and may start a family.

Finally, at about the age of 60, everyone enters the last and most sensitive Vata or V period of life. Many problems can arise during this period, as a result of getting older and because V is easily imbalanced at this time.

TO LIVE LONGER, Ayurveda recommends Four Simple Steps:

- Follow the Ayurvedic guidelines for better digestion
- Eat according to your Energy State
- Exercise regularly according to your Energy State
- Follow an Ayurvedic daily routine

THE NEUROPHYSIOLOGY OF TRANSFORMATION

How do you make a change or transformation in your life? Change usually requires a certain degree of energy, and you must also be prepared to take a new path, one which might conflict with your current habits. This means overcoming existing habits and even deeply rooted addictions in your physiology and neurochemistry.

Numerous experiments clearly show that *experience changes the brain*. When you learn to play a new musical instrument, for example, certain areas in the motor cortex become thicker. The brain is incredibly dynamic, with new synapses and pathways constantly being formed and supported by molecular changes in your neurons and supporting cells. And these may be initiated by changes in the expression of specific genes.

Behavioral changes are also influenced by your gut bacteria. You now know that your gut bacteria play an important role in weight gain or loss, and can even influence the brain pathways involved in eating disorders and alcohol and drug addiction.

So how do you make a change? Let's take a simple example: Say you are overweight and want to lose a few pounds. You may simply want to look better, or you might need to lose weight because your doctor tells you that obesity is a primary risk factor for diabetes and heart disease.

Is this motivation enough? Well, it's a beginning. The next step is to start to make some changes in your life, and change requires the rewiring of specific circuits or networks in your brain, as well as the rebooting of your microbiome. Some habits have been reinforced since early childhood and the neural networks and physiological patterns in your body have been present for a long time.

One positive habit change can stimulate a series of further changes in a sort of cascade. This is the definition of a Super Habit. If you learn to meditate, for example, or begin a certain kind of exercise program, it can then be easier to stop smoking, lose weight, and make other positive lifestyle changes.

Ayurveda suggests that you make small changes slowly in the beginning and understand that it will take time before the change really "sticks." If you consider that your habits are based on physical neural circuits in your brain and/or a disruption in your microbiome, you will understand that these complex physical systems take time to change. New, alternative circuits have to be created in your brain, and healing your gut lining and rebooting your microbiome will nourish and support this process.

We have offered you some basic tools so that you can immediately begin to take small steps forward in your process of change. And we encourage you to take advantage of every health resource available to you in your journey of transformation to a new level of health and happiness.

Remember, food is medicine and a few simple changes in your lifestyle and eating habits will naturally help improve every aspect of your physical and mental health.

SECTION 7

Health Coaching

The current profession of health coaching ranges from helping to support patients in conventional hospitals, to working in an alternative wellness health setting with clients who are more interested in natural and traditional health care.

TBC health coaches use a unique, integrative approach that combines the time-tested knowledge of Ayurveda along with the latest scientific research in modern medicine. A TBC health coach will help clients create positive health habits, while educating them about the most effective personalized preventive programs.

TBC health coaching begins by establishing trust with the client. The coach helps the client identify realistic, healthy goals in areas such as diet, exercise, sleep, and stress management. Everyone is different. Using the Energy State assessment tool helps greatly.

One of the most important new areas in health is the

understanding of the gut-brain axis and its impact on all aspects of mental and physical wellbeing. TBC health coaches will provide the latest knowledge and how it relates to each Energy State.

To gain a more profound understanding of Ayurveda and Integrative Medicine, it is ideal for TBC health coaches to take the online Master's degree program in Maharishi AyurVeda and Integrative Medicine at Maharishi International University, in Fairfield, Iowa. One unique feature of this program is advanced training in Ayurveda pulse diagnosis (see Resource Materials Section 4).

MAHARISHI AYURVEDA DEGREE PROGRAMS

Maharishi AyurVeda is a revival of Ayurveda, which includes a profound understand of consciousness and Transcendental Meditation, as well as an advanced methodology of pulse diagnosis. Maharishi International University (MIU) was founded by Maharishi Mahesh Yogi, who is also the founder of the Transcendental Meditation technique, and Maharishi AyurVeda. MIU offers an online Master of Science degree in Maharishi AyurVeda and Integrative Medicine. The program is a 3-year part-time online program, which integrates the ancient knowledge of Ayurveda with what has been discovered by modern medicine. It is taught by qualified doctors, and students are given in-residence clinical training by Maharishi AyurVeda experts for two weeks each year. MIU is a member of the National Ayurvedic

Medical Association and is accredited by the Higher Learning Commission. MIU also offers an online and in-residence BA in Ayurveda Wellness and Integrative Health. See MIU.edu for more details.

TROUBLE IN PARADISE

SECTION 8

Beauty and Essential Oil Skincare

Samantha Wallace, Robert Keith Wallace, PhD, and Veronica Butler, MD, have written *Beauty, Ayurveda, and Essential Oil Skincare—A Friendly Introduction*. The book includes a Quiz to determine your True Skin Type, and explains how understanding your True Skin Type provides you with an extraordinarily personal guide to caring for your skin, your health, and your inner and outer beauty at any age.

It is the authors' intention that after reading this book, you can look at the label of any skin product and be able to answer three important questions:

- *Does it contain oils that are good for my particular skin?*
- *Are the Essential Oils listed worth the price?*
- *Are there any chemicals I should check for toxicity?*

SECTION 9

Relationship Coaching

TBC Relationship Coaches help their clients become more empathetic and compatible, drop negative habits and form new positive ones. The coach will also encourage realizable goals for a loving and harmonious relationship.

In order to have a meaningful relationship, the client must understand Energy States and how they interact. This will give them the necessary understanding of the common triggers which lead to misunderstandings and blow-ups.

The examples below are illustrations of interactions that may occur between specific Energy State partners.

A TBC coach will learn to be aware of the nature of these interactions and have the tools necessary to improve the relationship.

V Partner / V Partner

When a balanced V Energy State person has a relationship with another balanced V partner, they will probably be very compatible and get great joy from each other's creativity. Since they are both extremely sensitive, however, if one of them goes out of balance, any slight misunderstanding on either side can cause hurt feelings. If both V Energy State partners go out of balance, their life can become an emotional tornado.

ADVICE:
Both V partners need to stay grounded. V Energy State individuals dislike routines, but the right routine will help to stabilize both their emotions and their physiology, and allow them to be their best selves. V people do not do well in cold and wind and should avoid them as much as possible. (At the very least they need to seriously bundle up well in such conditions.) Sipping hot water throughout the day is a simple but powerful way to help balance V Energy and help prevent illness. Daily warm oil self-massage with a balancing V oil will also help. The master tool for inner and outer balance is, of course, meditation.

P Partner / P Partner

Two P Energy State partners equals fire x 2! But this potentially combustible combination works very well when they are both in good balance because they both have a lot of energy and are highly motivated. They also love competition, physical exercise, and challenges.

ADVICE:
It is critically important that neither P partner misses a meal or becomes overheated! If either of them goes out of balance, arguments and a power struggle will surely follow. Both of them need to understand exactly what triggers a P Energy State outburst. Prevention is key.

K Partner / K Partner

K Energy State partners are like two contented teddy bears. Being on time is never an issue because they have the same slow, steady inner rhythm. If either one of them goes out of balance, however, stubbornness and depression may follow, straining the relationship.

ADVICE:
K people need to get out, get energized, and interact socially. This prescription includes a daily dose of active exercise.

If both Ks go out of balance, they may need outside help from a coach or trusted friend.

V Partner / P Partner

This can be an amazing relationship. The P Energy State partner is powerful, highly energetic, and driven. The V Energy State partner is sensitive, responsive, and artistic. The hot, fiery P is complemented by the cool, airy V. But when the P person goes out of balance, internal fires can flare out of control and damage the feelings of the vulnerable V. When they both go out of balance, the relationship may become an emotionally destructive inferno.

ADVICE:
In this relationship especially, both partners have to focus on staying in good balance. Even then, the P partner must be careful not to be too overbearing or controlling.

The V partner has to be careful to stay in balance in order not to become too overly sensitive and reactive.

V Partner / K Partner

This pair of opposites often makes for an ideal relationship. The calm, easygoing nature of the K partner enjoys and balances the volatile, talkative V partner.

When they both are in good balance, their different operating speeds don't matter. If, however, either one of them goes out of balance, their differences can suddenly result in an argument over even small things.

ADVICE:

The V partner is the more sensitive, so the K partner has to help the V stay well rested and on a good routine.

If the K partner goes out of balance, then the V partner will have to use some energy and strength to help the K get back on track. It is much, much easier for both of them to take *preventive* rather than remedial steps to ensure that they stay in balance!

P Partner / K Partner

A P partner in good balance is always motivated towards action and enjoys the challenges of life, while the K partner is calm and capable of handling even the most difficult situations. It is an excellent combination until one of them goes out of balance and the situation falls apart. The P partner will very quickly become intense and controlling, and probably become impatient and angry. The imbalanced K partner is more likely to become withdrawn and stubborn, and difficult to communicate with.

ADVICE:

Some of The P partner's great energy has to be directed towards helping the K partner continue to be active and in good balance.

The natural kindness and steady nature of the K partner must help to make sure that the P partner eats on time and stays cool!

SECTION 10

Parental Coaching

Total Brain or TBC parent coaching is designed to help parents improve their own habits, and teaches them how to help their children to also form good habits. The tools of TBC parent coaching can be found in the book *Dharma Parenting*. The word "dharma" is used in this context to mean a way of living that maintains balance, supports both prosperity and spiritual values, and unfolds the highest path of individual development. The TBC parenting tools make it easier to resolve problems in the deeply rewarding but challenging world of parenthood.

As a TBC parent coach, you will help parents understand why one child learns quickly and forgets quickly, while another learns slowly and forgets slowly; why one child is hyperactive and another slow; why one falls asleep quickly but wakes in the night and another takes hours to fall asleep. Total Brain Coaching gives parents the tools they need to help unfold the full potential of their child's brain and nurture their inherent brilliance and goodness.

The first tool of TBC parent coaching is to determine their children's Energy State and identify factors that can cause it to go out of balance. Of course, it is also important to determine the Energy State of the parent and help them to stay in balance so they can avoid obvious conflicts with their children. The following is adapted from the book *Dharma Parenting*:

THE V OR VATA PARENT

As a V Energy State parent, your strengths are your creativity, flexibility, and your lightheartedness. When a problem arises, you can usually figure out several possible solutions to choose from. Your kids love how you sometimes whisk them off on spur-of-the-moment adventures. But V parents don't always have enough stamina for the intense 24/7 focus and resolve that parenting requires. You may find that your V mind is going in a million directions at once, your anxiety is peaking, and your energy level is dropping fast. This is why you, more than any other brain/body or Energy type, need to figure out how you can take a break to settle your wild V physiology down, and generally re-energize and regroup. Maybe you can arrange for everyone in the house to take a period of quiet time, with Vata aromatherapy, soothing music, and comfy cushions to lie around on. And if you have learned Transcendental Meditation, take twenty minutes to do it twice a day, even if you have to wait until everyone else is in bed. TM is your most powerful tool to keep your V balanced so you can be at your best.

THE P OR PITTA PARENT

As a P Energy State parent, your strengths are your physical energy, warmth, organizational ability, and intelligence. Your lively intellect can stimulate your children's curiosity about the world, and your warm heart and sense of responsibility gives them a sense of security and being loved. Of all the Energy States, you are certainly the most proactive. Because you are good at (and enjoy) solving problems and planning ahead, you naturally visualize problems before they arise and figure out how to avoid them. But your P focus may be too strong—you can get so caught up in the task at hand that you are unaware of, or may even disregard, the feelings of those around you, or you overlook a family situation that needs your immediate attention, in favor of some interesting professional problem. And if your P Energy State becomes aggravated by overheating, delayed meals, spicy foods, or someone challenging your authority, the extra heat will probably set off explosions.

Of all the types, Ps most need to keep their cool. Do not allow yourself to get hungry or thirsty. You can see that these things aggravate your P child, and of course, they do the same to you.

Plan outdoor summer activities in the cool of the morning or evening. If your child's T-ball game or tennis match is at noon, wear a hat, try for a seat in the shade, and keep your bottle of cool water handy. Ice cream or a milkshake afterward is not only a treat but will help cool you down. P Energy State aromatherapy, especially at night, can help. If you think that you might have to deal with a potential confrontation—negotiating with your teenager about prom night, for example—plan to do it only after a good meal when everyone is fed and rested. Offer cool drinks.

THE K OR KAPHA PARENT

As a K Energy State parent, you provide stability, strength, and loving comfort in your children's life. You are the bedrock, the foundation of their world. With your calm steadiness, you can structure and maintain a stable routine that provides a secure framework for their growth. And your stamina helps you ride out the ups and downs of parenting. But if you go beyond your limits of endurance, fatigue can drag that steadiness down into inertia, and your wonderful calmness can degrade to passivity and emotional withdrawal. It is important for you to carve some "off duty" time into your schedule in order for you to regroup and relax. While you would rather opt for watching your favorite movie, remember that K types are usually happier and more nourished when making or moving. Useful projects requiring painstaking work, or crafts such as woodworking or sewing, will satisfy you more than passive entertainment.

K Energy State people have a tendency to become sedentary, so make it a point to keep yourself enlivened. Exercise is very important to keep your sturdy physiology from becoming sluggish and overweight. And if you can exercise as a group activity, that can be more ideal for you. It doesn't have to be aerobics or calisthenics—a wild game of tag, a brisk walk, or shooting hoops can get your family involved. Lighter foods—think fruit instead of cake, tortilla chips and popcorn instead of fries—will also help. And you are the one Energy State who does well with tasty, spicy food! Remember that even though K Energy people are hard to get started, they are much more balanced and therefore happier, when they finally get moving. Do whatever you have to do—even trick yourself if necessary to start an exercise program, finish a painting, put an addition on your house, or get going on that upholstery project you've been thinking about—anything which will help keep your K Energy State active and in good balance and help you to be a better parent.

SECTION 11

Group Dynamics of Consciousness

GROUP PRACTICE OF TRANSCENDENTAL MEDITATION AND MORE ADVANCED TECHNIQUES

The collective consciousness of any company or any group of people is the sum of the consciousness of all of the individuals in that company or group. When the collective consciousness is incoherent, the company will almost certainly lack a clear mission and have many internal problems. When the collective consciousness is coherent, the company will have a unified mission—a clear intention of its purpose—and will demonstrate optimal teamwork and performance.

The concept of a collective consciousness which underlies and influences the structure of society has been expressed by many great thinkers. Some sophisticated sociological theories have vaguely described it as a social field or an interlocking network of social and behavioral interactions within specific economic and environmental conditions.

Maharishi Mahesh Yogi, founder of the Transcendental Meditation technique, was the first to encourage scientific research on the concept of collective consciousness. Many scientific papers, published in peer-reviewed journals, verify the practical application of Maharishi's concepts. Many of the comments about the group dynamics of consciousness can be found in Maharishi's books.

In 1960, Maharishi predicted that one percent of a population practicing the Transcendental Meditation technique would produce measurable improvements in the quality of life for the whole population. This phenomenon was first studied in 1974 and was referred to as the "Maharishi Effect." In 1976, Maharishi brought out several advanced programs derived from the Vedic tradition, which greatly enhanced the Maharishi Effect. Scientists found that when even the square root of one percent of any population practices these programs in a group, there is a measurable marked reduction in violence and an improvement in the quality of life, a type of macroscopic field effect of coherence.

A large number of studies have documented the beneficial effects of the practice of TM and its advanced programs on reducing crime and violence and improving the quality of life in different areas of the world. One demonstration project was conducted in

1993 in Washington, DC, by Dr. John Hagelin and colleagues. An independent panel of more than twenty sociologists, criminologists, and members of the Washington, DC government and police department advised on the study design and reviewed the analysis of the findings. The study included over 4000 people gathered in Washington to participate in a "peace assembly," practicing TM and specific related advanced programs for extended periods. Results showed that as the group size increased, there was a highly significant decrease in violent crime.

A remarkable aspect of this study was that it took place in the summer, when the weather is especially hot in Washington. In fact, the police chief of Washington, who sat on the independent board of researchers monitoring the project, said in an interview, "The only way this group can lower crime by 20 percent in Washington in August is if we have two feet of snow!" In fact, the meditating group lowered crime by 23.6 percent.

How could such a thing happen? The individuals in the group didn't go out on the streets and physically stop people from committing crimes. They simply meditated quietly together in various locations around the city. The coherence effect which they created in the collective consciousness of the city was similar to the result of throwing a pebble in a pond: ripples of higher, more coherent waves of consciousness went out in all directions, creating sufficient coherence in the collective consciousness of the city so that crime was spontaneously reduced.

Research demonstrates that it is possible to influence the collective consciousness of society through the group practice of the TM technique and its advanced programs.

Selected References on the Group Dynamics of Consciousness

Hagelin JS, et al. Effects of group practice of the Transcendental Meditation program on preventing violent crime in Washington, DC: results of the National Demonstration Project, June-July 1993. *Social Indicators Research* 47: 153-201, 1999

Orme-Johnson DW, et al. International peace project in the Middle East: The effect of the Maharishi Technology of the Unified Field. *Journal of Conflict Resolution* 32: 776–812, 1988

Orme-Johnson DW, et al. The long-term effects of the Maharishi Technology of the Unified Field on the quality of life in the United States (1960 to 1983). *Social Science Perspectives Journal* 2:127-146, 1988

Orme-Johnson DW, et al. Preventing terrorism and international conflict: Effects of large assemblies of participants in the Transcendental Meditation and TM-Sidhi programs. *Journal of Offender Rehabilitation* 36: 283–302, 2003

Brown CL. Overcoming barriers to use of promising research among elite Middle East policy groups. *Journal of Social Behavior and Personality* 17:489-546, 2005

Cavanaugh KL. Time series analysis of U.S. and Canadian inflation and unemployment: A test of a field-theoretic hypothesis. *Proceedings of the American Statistical Association, Business and Economics*

Statistics Section (Alexandria, VA: American Statistical Association): 799–804, 1987

Cavanaugh KL, King KD. Simultaneous transfer function analysis of Okun's misery index: Improvements in the economic quality of life through Maharishi's Vedic Science and technology of consciousness. *Proceedings of the American Statistical Association, Business and Economics Statistics Section* (Alexandria, VA: American Statistical Association): 491–496, 1988

Davies JL. Alleviating political violence through enhancing coherence in collective consciousness. *Dissertation Abstracts International* 49(8): 2381A, 1989

Gelderloos P, et al. The dynamics of US–Soviet relations, 1979–1986: Effects of reducing social stress through the Transcendental Meditation and TM-Sidhi program. *Proceedings of the Social Statistics Section of the American Statistical Association* (Alexandria, VA: American Statistical Association): 297–302, 1990

Dillbeck MC. Test of a field theory of consciousness and social change: Time series analysis of participation in the TM-Sidhi program and reduction of violent death in the U.S. *Social Indicators Research* 22: 399–418, 1990

Assimakis PD, Dillbeck MC. Time series analysis of improved quality of life in Canada: Social change, collective consciousness, and the TM-Sidhi program. *Psychological Reports* 76: 1171–1193, 1995

Hatchard GD, et al. A model for social improvement. Time series analysis of a phase transition to reduced crime in Merseyside metropolitan area. *Psychology, Crime, and Law* 2: 165–174, 1996

Dillbeck MC, et al. The Transcendental Meditation program and crime rate change in a sample of forty-eight cities. *Journal of Crime and Justice* 4: 25–45, 1981

Dillbeck MC, et al. Test of a field model of consciousness and social change: The Transcendental Meditation and TM-Sidhi program and decreased urban crime. *The Journal of Mind and Behavior* 9: 457–486, 1988

Dillbeck MC. et al. Consciousness as a field: The Transcendental Meditation and TM-Sidhi program and changes in social indicators. *The Journal of Mind and Behavior* 8: 67–104, 1987.

SECTION 12

David Lynch Foundation

The David Lynch Foundation for education and world peace is a global charitable foundation founded by film director David Lynch. The Foundation aims to prevent and eradicate trauma and stress among at-risk populations through promoting widespread implementation of the evidence-based Transcendental Meditation program in order to improve their health, cognitive capabilities and performance in life.

At-risk populations suffer from epidemic levels of chronic stress and stress-related disorders—fueling violence, crime, and soaring health costs, and compromising the effectiveness of education, health, rehabilitation and vocational programs now in place. Since its founding in 2005, the David Lynch Foundation, a 501(c)(3) organization, has helped to bring the stress-reducing Transcendental Meditation technique to more than 500,000 children and adults around the world. The Foundation focuses on underserved inner-city students; veterans with PTSD and their families; and women and children who are survivors of violence and abuse.

The David Lynch Foundation has organized and hosted scientific and professional conferences on business, education, veterans, corrections, and rehabilitation as well as "town hall" meetings to educate leaders and the general public in the benefits of Transcendental Meditation. In addition, the Foundation funds university and medical school research to assess the effects of the program on academic performance, ADHD and other learning disorders, anxiety, depression, substance abuse, cardiovascular disease, post-traumatic stress disorder, and diabetes.

The Foundation has worked with other private foundations and government agencies, including the National Institutes of Health, General Motors Foundation, the Chrysler Foundation, the Kellogg Foundation, the American Indian Education Association, and Indian Health Services, along with numerous school districts and state departments of corrections.

[Note to Reader: The TM program has been endorsed and supported by a number of well-known individuals including Tom Hanks, Martin Scorsese, Ellen DeGeneres, Jerry Seinfeld, Paul McCartney, George Stephanopoulos, Katy Perry, and Hugh Jackman, among many others.]

GENERAL REFERENCES

USEFUL WEBSITES

Totalbraincoaching.com
TM.org
MIU.edu
Coherenceeffect.com

USEFUL BOOKS

Coaching

Total Brain Coaching: A Holistic System of Effective Habit Change For the Individual, Team, and Organization by Ted Wallace, MS, Robert Keith Wallace, PhD, and Samantha Wallace, Dharma Publications, 2020

The Smith Saga

Trouble in Paradise—A Humorous Story: Change Your Habits In 7 Steps with Total Brain Coaching by Robert Keith Wallace, PhD, Samantha Wallace, Ted Wallace, MS, Dharma Publications, 2020

Quantum Golf: The Path to Golf Mastery by Kjell Enhager and Samantha Wallace, Warner Books, New York, 1991

The Coherence Code: How to Maximize Your Performance And Success in Business—For Individuals, Teams, and Organizations by Robert Keith Wallace, PhD, Ted Wallace, MS, Samantha Wallace, Dharma Publications, 2020

Beauty, Ayurveda, and Essential Oil Skincare—A Friendly Introduction by Samantha Wallace, Robert Keith Wallace, PhD and Veronica Wells Butler, MD, in press

Habit Change

Tiny Habits: The Small Changes That Change Everything by BJ Fogg, Houghton Mifflin Harcourt, 2019

The Power of Habit: Why We Do What We Do in Life and Business by Charles Duhigg, Random House, 2012

Atomic Habits: An Easy & Proven Way to Build Good Habits & Break Bad Ones by James Clear, Avery, 2018

Triggers: Creating Behavior That Lasts—Becoming the Person You Want to Be by Marshall Goldsmith and Mark Reiter, Crown Business, 2015

Balancing Your Energy State

Gut Crisis: How Diet, Probiotics, and Friendly Bacteria Help You Lose Weight and Heal Your Body and Mind by Robert Keith Wallace, PhD, and Samantha Wallace, Dharma Publications, 2017

The Rest And Repair Diet: Heal Your Gut, Improve Your Physical and Mental Health, and Lose Weight by Robert Keith Wallace, PhD, Samantha Wallace, Andrew Stenberg, MA, Jim Davis, DO, and Alexis Farley, Dharma Publications, 2019

Dharma Parenting: Understand Your Child's Brilliant Brain for Greater Happiness, Health, Success, and Fulfillment by Robert Keith Wallace, PhD, and Frederick Travis, PhD, Tarcher/Perigree, 2016

Creating Coherence

The Coherence Effect: Tapping into the Laws of Nature that Govern Health, Happiness, and Higher Brain Functioning by Robert Keith Wallace, PhD, Jay B. Marcus and Chris S. Clark, MD, Armin Lear Press, 2020

Transcendental Meditation and Maharishi AyurVeda

Science of Being and Art of Living: Transcendental Meditation by Maharishi Mahesh Yogi, MUM Press, Kindle edition, 2011

Maharishi Mahesh Yogi on the Bhagavad-Gita, A New Translation and Commentary, Chapters 1-6, MUM Press, 2016

Strength in Stillness: The Power of Transcendental Meditation by Bob Roth, Simon & Schuster, 2018

Catching the Big Fish: Meditation, Consciousness, and Creativity by David Lynch, Tarcher/Penguin 2007

An Introduction to Transcendental Meditation: Improve Your Brain Functioning, Create Ideal Health, and Gain Enlightenment Naturally, Easily, Effortlessly by Robert Keith Wallace, PhD, and Lincoln Akin Norton, Dharma Publications, 2016

Transcendental Meditation: A Scientist's Journey to Happiness, Health, and Peace, Adapted and Updated from The Physiology of Consciousness: Part 1 by Robert Keith Wallace, PhD, Dharma Publications, 2016

The Neurophysiology of Enlightenment: How the Transcendental

Meditation and TM-Sidhi Program Transform the Functioning of the Human Body by Robert Keith Wallace, PhD, Dharma Publications, 2016

Maharishi Ayurveda and Vedic Technology: Creating Ideal Health for the Individual and World, Adapted and Updated from The Physiology of Consciousness: Part 2 by Robert Keith Wallace, PhD, Dharma Publications, 2016

In Balance leben: Wie wir trotz Stress mit unserer Energie richtig umgehen Broschiert (Translation: Living in Balance: How to deal with our energy properly despite stress) by Dr. med. Ulrich Bauhofer, Südwest Verlag, 2013

Business Performance

Success from Within: Discovering the Inner State that Creates Personal Fulfillment and Business Success by Jay B. Marcus, MIU Press, 1990

Enlightened Management: Building High-Performance People by Gerald Swanson and Bob Oates, MIU Press, 1987

Principles: Life and Work by Ray Dalio, Simon & Schuster, 2017

World-Class Brain by Harald Harung, PhD and Frederick Travis, PhD, Harvest, AS, 2019

DAVID LYNCH FOUNDATION

Index

A

action 35, 53, 58, 70, 102
addiction 64, 79, 183
amygdala 111
attention 26, 31, 32, 58, 59, 60, 61, 62, 63, 65, 70, 71, 77, 79, 85, 86, 87, 91, 106, 121, 158, 163, 201
Ayurgenomics 14, 153
Ayurveda v, 1, 10, 13, 14, 37, 49, 72, 74, 75, 112, 135, 140, 152, 155, 156, 175, 180, 182, 184, 187, 188, 189, 191, 214, 216

B

balance 11, 14, 22, 27, 29, 30, 48, 49, 50, 60, 62, 63, 66, 70, 72, 74, 75, 76, 83, 84, 87, 88, 91, 92, 93, 96, 97, 98, 99, 108, 145, 146, 147, 148, 149, 150, 151, 152, 171, 174, 177, 194, 195, 196, 197, 199, 200, 203
beauty v, vii, 1, 13, 37, 140, 191, 214
Bhagavad-Gita 120, 125, 215
BJ Fogg 63, 175, 214

C

Charles Duhigg 56, 175, 214
coaching iv, vii, 35, 36, 46, 47, 58, 66, 67, 70, 73, 74, 75, 76, 77, 79, 82, 140, 177, 199, 213
coherence iv, v, 1, 3, 14, 29, 36, 37, 132, 135, 136, 140, 214, 215
Coherence Code iv, 1, 3, 14, 29, 36, 37, 136, 140, 214
collective consciousness 136, 205, 206, 207, 208, 209
cortisol 111, 160

D

Damage Control 116, 117, 118, 125

Dame Georgina 3, 9, 11, 25, 27, 28, 29, 36, 46, 56, 65, 83, 86, 90, 136
David Lynch Foundation viii, 211, 212
DHARMIC 46, 47, 53, 54, 58, 65, 66, 67, 69, 70, 73, 74, 76, 77
diet iv, 13, 14, 92, 94, 140, 152, 163, 170, 180, 214
digestion 92, 179
Discover Yourself 47, 53
dopamine 78

E

Energy State 14, 96, 98
Energy State Quiz 11, 15
Energy States 11, 13, 14, 17, 54, 60, 62, 66, 70, 71, 84, 92, 93, 151, 173, 182, 193, 201
environment 13, 28, 55, 62, 66, 72, 76, 93, 136, 175, 176
exercise 94, 181, 183, 203

F

feedback 75, 77, 78, 79
Fred Travis 126

G

Group Dynamics of Consciousness vii, 205, 208
gut bacteria 74, 169, 183
gut-brain axis 55, 92, 169, 188

H

habit 27, 29, 37, 46, 54, 55, 56, 59, 60, 63, 64, 65, 66, 69, 70, 71, 72, 73, 74, 75, 76, 77, 78, 79, 89, 91, 175, 176, 177, 184
Habit Map 35, 47, 53, 54, 176, 177
Habit Map and Plan 35, 53, 177
habit stacking 72, 175
happiness 78, 79, 157, 181, 182, 185
hippocampus 111

I

imbalance 14, 48, 148, 171

J

James Clear 175, 214

K

karma 43, 48, 59, 102
K Energy State 17, 30, 31, 48, 60, 62, 74, 85, 92, 93, 98, 146, 148, 149, 152, 153, 173, 174, 177, 195, 202, 203
keystone habit 56

L

Linc St. Claire 3, 36, 56, 83, 89

M

Maharishi AyurVeda 76, 188, 215
Maharishi Effect. 206
Maharishi International University 139, 140, 188
Maintaining Balance 74, 91
Marshall Goldsmith 77, 175, 214
meditation 20, 48, 49, 56, 64, 65, 74, 75, 88, 95, 125, 126, 158, 159, 162, 164, 181, 194
microbiome 155, 169, 170, 180, 184
motivation 67, 78, 79, 91, 175, 184

N

neural circuits 89, 90, 184
neuroplasticity 54

P

parenting 71, 199, 200, 202
P Energy State 11, 16, 27, 29, 31, 47, 48, 59, 62, 63, 66, 71, 72, 73, 83, 84, 85, 88, 92, 93, 94, 95, 97, 98, 108, 115, 146, 147, 149, 153, 173, 174, 177, 194, 195, 196, 201, 202
performance 78, 91, 92, 152, 166, 205, 211, 212

Q

Q swing 24
Quantum Golf iv, 1, 3, 35, 37, 125, 140, 213

R

relationship vii, 65, 193
Rest And Repair Diet 13, 94, 140, 214

S

Self Pulse vii, 76, 91, 152, 171
sleep 16, 50, 74, 75, 87, 92, 98, 110, 150, 152, 181, 187
stress 95, 163, 165, 166, 216
styloid process 172
Super Habit 48, 56, 64, 72, 184

T

TBC Life Coaching 35, 47, 66, 67, 70, 73, 74, 76, 77, 79, 82
TM v, 49, 56, 65, 121, 125, 127, 135, 136, 157, 158, 159, 160, 161, 162, 164, 165, 201, 205, 206, 207, 208, 209, 210, 212, 213, 216
Total Brain Coaching iv, 35, 36, 46, 58, 75, 79, 140, 177, 193, 199, 213
Transcendental Meditation v, 49, 56, 65, 95, 121, 125, 126, 127, 139, 157, 158, 159, 161, 163, 164, 165, 166, 181, 188, 200, 206, 208, 209, 210, 211, 212, 215
Tri-Energy State 17
triggers 77, 175, 214

V

V Energy State 15, 30, 31, 48, 60, 62, 70, 84, 92, 95, 96, 145, 148, 149, 152, 153, 173, 174, 177, 194, 196, 200

Y

yoga 95, 181, 182